INDESIGN CS2

ROBERT SHUFFLEBOTHAM

D1318884

In easy steps is an imprint of Computer Step
Southfield Road · Southam
Warwickshire CV47 0FB · United Kingdom
www.ineasysteps.com

Notice of Liability
Every effort has been made to ensure that this book contains accurate and current information. However, Computer Step and the author shall not be liable for any loss or damage suffered by readers as a result of any information contained herein.

Trademarks
Adobe® and InDesign® are registered trademarks of Adobe Systems Incorporated. All other trademarks are acknowledged as belonging to their respective companies.

Printed and bound in the United Kingdom

ISBN 1-84078-304-4

Table of Contents

Paragraph Settings 71

Images and Graphic Frames 87

Arranging Objects 101

Working with Color 119

The Working Environment

Adobe InDesign is a page layout application that integrates tightly with both Adobe Photoshop and Adobe Illustrator. Using Adobe InDesign you can create anything from a simple leaflet through to complex publications such as magazines, newspapers and books.

This chapter takes a look at the working environment and gets you started using Adobe InDesign. It covers setting up a new document and introduces toolbox and palette conventions along with other useful techniques that will help make you accurate and productive as you start to use the software.

Covers

Chapter One

Document Setup

Launch Adobe InDesign as you would any other application (from the Start menu – Windows, or from the Applications folder or Dock – Mac). When the copyright screen and Toolbox appear you can create a new document.

Size and Orientation

1 To create a new document, choose File>New. The New Document dialog box appears. Use the Page Size drop-down list to choose a standard page size, if appropriate.

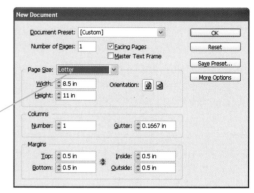

2 To create a non-standard page size, make sure the Width entry field is highlighted, and then enter the page width you require. Then, do the same with the Height entry field.

3 Click the Landscape icon if you want to create a landscape page orientation. Portrait is selected by default.

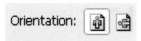

4 Enter the number of pages you want in the document. If you are unsure of the number of pages you need, you can always add or delete pages when you are working in the document.

...cont'd

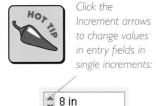

Click the Increment arrows to change values in entry fields in single increments:

To set the default measurement system for all new documents, launch InDesign, but do not start a new document. Choose Edit>Preferences>Units & Increments (Windows), or InDesign> Preferences>Units & Increments (Mac). Change the Horizontal and Vertical Ruler Units pop-up menu to the unit of measurement you want to use:

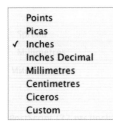

See page 28 for information on setting Margin and Column guides for specific pages or master pages after page setup.

5 Choose the Facing Pages option if you want to create a publication such as a magazine or brochure which will consist of double-page spreads. If you choose Facing Pages, Left and Right in the Margins area change to Inside and Outside, allowing you to set a wider inside margin to accommodate any binding edge in your document.

Margin Guides

Set margin guides to define the main text area of your document. Margin guides are non-printing and appear as magenta lines on the page. Margin guides are only guides – objects can be placed across margin guides or completely outside the margin guides.

1 Either enter values for Top, Bottom, Left/Right, Inside/Outside.

2 Or click the "Make all settings the same" button (🔒) to make it active, and then enter a value in one of the Margin entry fields. Press the Tab key to make all values the same as the first value you enter.

Column Guides

Column guides appear on screen as purple, non-printing guides and serve as a grid for constructing a publication. You are not constrained to working within the columns – all InDesign objects can cross column guides as necessary to create the page design you require.

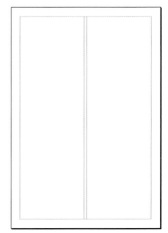

1 Enter the number of columns you want. Specify a Gutter – the space between columns. InDesign calculates the widths of columns based on the overall width of the page, the number of columns, and the values entered for margins and gutters.

The Working Environment

In common with Adobe Photoshop and Adobe Illustrator, Adobe InDesign is virtually identical on both the Windows and Macintosh platforms, making it easy to work in both environments without the need for extensive retraining.

This book uses a mixture of Windows and Macintosh screen shots, and the instructions given apply equally to both platforms. The identical functionality of InDesign on both platforms can be seen from an examination of the application windows on these pages, and from a comparison of the screen shots of various Windows and Macintosh dialog boxes and palettes throughout the book.

Command (often referred to as "Apple" on the Mac) and Ctrl (Windows), and Alt/option (Mac) and Alt (Windows) are used identically as modifier keys. Shift is standard on both platforms.

This book uses Alt, with an uppercase "A", to denote both the Macintosh and Windows keys of that name.

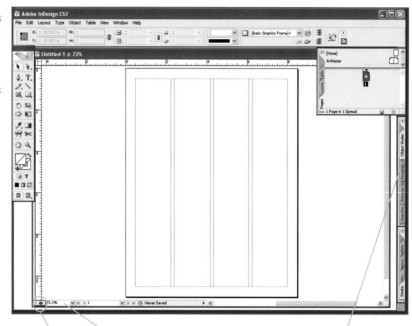

Windows users can use the right mouse button to access context-sensitive menus; Mac users can hold down the control key and press their single mouse button.

Click the Show/ Hide Structure button to expand/ collapse the XML structure pane.

Double-click the View Percentage field to highlight the existing value. Enter a new value; then press Enter/ Return to change the magnification level.

The Palette bar runs down the right edge of the InDesign window.

Drag the Zero Point crosshairs onto the page to reset the zero point.

The file name of the document appears in the Title Bar after you save it.

Drag the Title Bar to reposition the InDesign window.

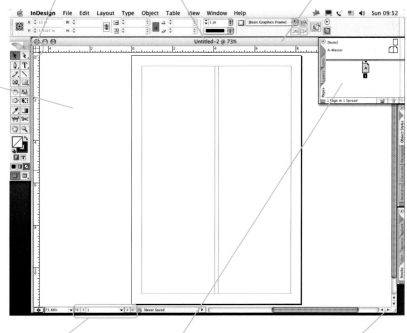

The Pasteboard area exists all around the document page or spread.

Objects you place on the Pasteboard are saved with the document but do not print. To avoid any confusion, it is good practice to delete unnecessary items from the pasteboard before you send your document to a commercial printer.

The Page Controls allow you to move to the Next/Previous, First/Last pages in a multi-page document, or any page you specify in the Page Number field.

The first time you launch InDesign, the Pages palette is visible so that you are aware of the presence of the various palette tabs in the Palette bar on the extreme right of the screen.

Click the Scroll Arrows to scroll the page up, down, left or right in increments. You can drag the Scroll Box to move the page a custom amount. Alternatively, click either side of the Scroll Box to move the window in half-screen increments.

Each time you launch InDesign the Welcome screen appears. Click one of the listed links, or click the Close button to begin working in InDesign. To prevent the Welcome screen appearing every time you launch InDesign, deselect the Show this dialog at startup checkbox.

Opening Documents

In Windows, InDesign documents have the extension .indd. InDesign templates have the extension .indt.

As well as creating new InDesign documents, you will often need to open existing documents. InDesign can open documents created in InDesign itself, Adobe PageMaker 6.5 or later and QuarkXPress v3.3–4.1x. You use the same procedure to open files of all the above types.

1 To open an existing document, choose File>Open.

In the Open a File dialog box, click the Copy radio button to open a copy of the file – the file opens as an untitled document.

2 Use standard Windows/ Mac techniques to navigate to the file you want to open.

When you want to edit a template, in the Open a File dialog box, click on the template file name and then select the Original radio button before you click Open.

3 Click the file name to select it. Click the Open button.

Converting QuarkXPress and PageMaker Files

InDesign can convert files created in QuarkXPress v3.3–4.1x and PageMaker 6.5 or later into Adobe InDesign files. To convert a QuarkXPress v5 or later file, open it in QuarkXPress and then resave it as a version 4 file.

InDesign does not support objects created or manipulated by, or dependent on, third party QuarkXTensions.

1 To open a file created originally in QuarkXPress or PageMaker choose File> Open.

2 Use standard Windows/Mac techniques to navigate to the file you want to open.

Check colors carefully after you open a QuarkXPress or PageMaker file: some color conversions may occur, depending on the color model used in the original file.

When converting complex QuarkXPress documents, such as magazine or book templates, read any conversion warnings carefully. InDesign may not be able to convert every single QuarkXPress feature with complete accuracy, and the alerts given in the warning dialog box can be useful as you fine-tune the converted files in InDesign.

If the QuarkXPress file you are converting contains linked image files, results will be best if you copy the linked files to the same folder as the QuarkXPress file before you convert it into an InDesign document.

3 (Windows) When opening a QuarkXPress or PageMaker file,

use the Files of Type pop-up to choose the appropriate file format. (Mac) Choose All Readable Documents from the Enable pop-up menu.

4 Click the file name to select it; then click the Open button. When you open a QuarkXPress or PageMaker file in Adobe InDesign

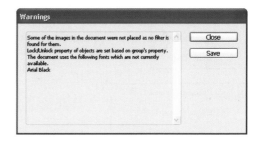

it opens as an untitled document. InDesign displays a warning message listing any objects or elements that cannot be converted to InDesign objects. Click the Save button to save a copy of the warning as a text file before opening the document in InDesign. Click Close to close the warning box. A progress bar appears, indicating which original elements are being converted into the native InDesign format.

5 As the document is an untitled document, save the file as an InDesign document before you proceed to work on it.

The Toolbox

Use the following techniques to choose tools and to work quickly and efficiently as you build page layouts in Adobe InDesign.

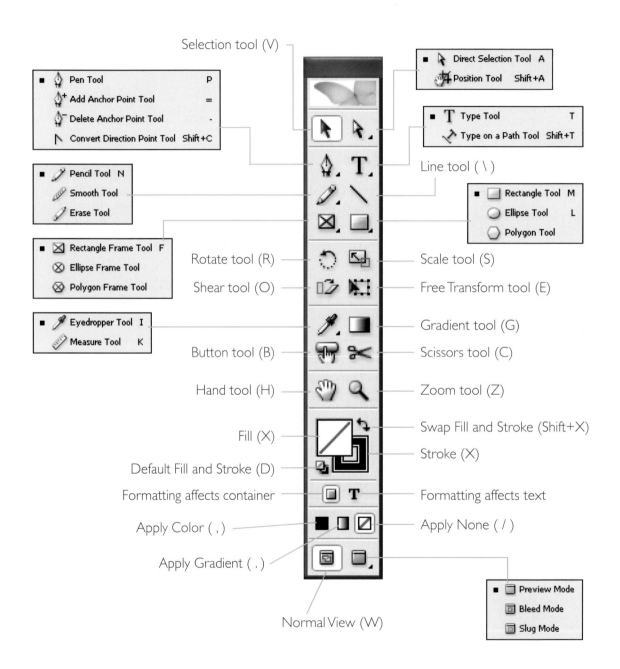

Selection tool (V)

- Pen Tool   P
- Add Anchor Point Tool   =
- Delete Anchor Point Tool   -
- Convert Direction Point Tool   Shift+C

- Direct Selection Tool   A
- Position Tool   Shift+A

- Type Tool   T
- Type on a Path Tool   Shift+T

Line tool (\ )

- Pencil Tool   N
- Smooth Tool
- Erase Tool

- Rectangle Tool   M
- Ellipse Tool   L
- Polygon Tool

- Rectangle Frame Tool   F
- Ellipse Frame Tool
- Polygon Frame Tool

Rotate tool (R)
Scale tool (S)

Shear tool (O)
Free Transform tool (E)

- Eyedropper Tool   I
- Measure Tool   K

Gradient tool (G)

Button tool (B)
Scissors tool (C)

Hand tool (H)
Zoom tool (Z)

Fill (X)
Swap Fill and Stroke (Shift+X)

Stroke (X)

Default Fill and Stroke (D)

Formatting affects container
Formatting affects text

Apply Color (,)
Apply None (/)

Apply Gradient (.)

Normal View (W)

- Preview Mode
- Bleed Mode
- Slug Mode

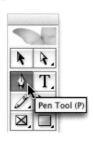

1 Most of the time you will have the Toolbox visible as you build documents. If you accidentally close it, choose Window>Tools to display the Toolbox.

2 To choose a tool, click on it in the Toolbox. The tool is highlighted and when you move your cursor back into the InDesign window, the cursor changes to indicate the tool you selected.

3 A small, black triangle in the bottom-right corner of a tool icon indicates that there are additional tools available in the tool group. To access a hidden tool, press and hold the tool currently showing in the Toolbox; this will show the tool group pop-up. Slide your cursor onto the tool you want to select, and then release. The tool you select is displayed in the Toolbox as the default tool in that group until you choose another tool from the group.

4 Provided that you do not have the text insertion point located in text, press the Tab key to hide all visible palettes including the Toolbox. Press Tab again to show all previously visible palettes. Hold down Shift and press the Tab key to hide all palettes except the Toolbox.

5 PageMaker users starting to use InDesign may find it useful to show the PageMaker toolbar (Window>PageMaker Toolbar). Click a button to access the InDesign equivalent of the PageMaker palette or dialog box:

Adobe Bridge

Adobe Bridge is a file management window providing a powerful, flexible set of controls which allow you to locate, track, view and manage all your digital assets created using Adobe CS2 applications as well as files created by other software applications. Click the Go to Bridge button in the Control palette to launch Adobe Bridge.

1   Click the Adobe Stock Photos panel to search online for images from stock photo libraries. A search area opens where you can enter keywords or Image IDs to begin your search.

2   The Recent Folders pane lists the most recent folders used by Creative Suite applications on your computer. Click a folder icon to display the contents.

3   The Recent Files pane lists the most recent files used by applications on your computer. Click a file icon to open the file. If the appropriate application is not running, Bridge launches it and opens the file so that you can work on it.

4   If you are working with files in different applications which are part of the same project, and the files are currently open, you can use Bridge to create a file group. This brings together the related files and makes it easy to locate and manage all the files in a project.

...cont'd

You can launch Adobe Bridge as a standalone application, as you would launch any other application – from the Start>Programs menu in Windows, or from the Applications folder on the Mac.

File Browser View

In File Browser view you can view, manage, sort and open files. You can also rename, move, delete and rank files.

1. In the Adobe Bridge window, click the Folder tab. Use the Folder pane to navigate to specific folders on your system using standard Windows/Macintosh techniques. You can also use the drop down list to navigate quickly to recently used folders.

Choose an option from the View>Sort sub-menu to control the way image thumbnails are ordered in the Preview pane:

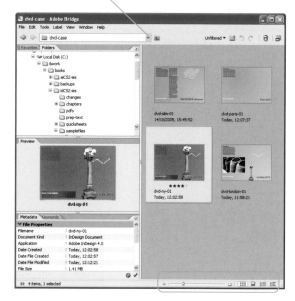

2. Thumbnail previews of the contents of the selected folder appear in the contents area on the right of the window.

3. Drag the Thumbnail Size slider to increase or decrease the size of the thumbnail previews. Use the View buttons to control the arrangement of the thumbnails.

To move a file, position your cursor on the image thumbnail, then drag it to a different folder in the Folder pane of the Adobe Bridge window. To copy a file to a new location, hold down Alt/option, then drag it to a different folder.

4. Click once on a file in the contents area to display a larger preview in the preview area. Position your cursor on any of the borders of the Preview pane, then drag to resize the pane as required.

...cont'd

5   To open a file from the content area, click on an image thumbnail to select it, and then press Enter/Return. You can also double-click on a thumbnail. Hold down Alt/option and double-click a thumbnail to open the file and close the Adobe Bridge window at the same time.

To display thumbnails in the content area according to their rank, choose View>Sort>By Rating.

6   To delete a file, click on the thumbnail to select it, and either click the Wastebasket icon in the Bridge Toolbar, or drag the thumbnail onto the Wastebasket. Alternatively, press the Delete key.

7   To rank a thumbnail, first select it; then click the leftmost dot below the thumbnail image to convert it to a star. You can add up to five stars. To remove one, click the star to the left of the final star.

8   To display only thumbnails with a specific star rating or higher, select an option from the Filter pop-up menu.

An open file icon appears with the thumbnail if the document is already open in an application:

9   Click the Metadata or Keywords tab to view additional labeling information saved with a file. You can also use options from the palette menu for each tab to add and edit metadata and keyword information for the file. Use the Expand/Collapse triangle to display/hide information for each category.

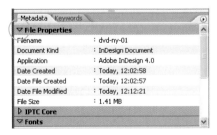

The Control Palette

As with other palettes and dialog boxes in InDesign, if you make a change to a setting with nothing selected, that setting becomes the default for objects you subsequently create. For example, if you use options in the Control palette to change the font to Arial and the type size to 72pt, the next time you create a text frame, any text you enter appears with these settings This is a useful and powerful feature of InDesign, but in the early stages of learning the application you have to be careful that it doesn't catch you out.

The Control palette is one of the most versatile palettes in InDesign. It provides convenient access to an extensive range of settings and controls. The controls available change depending on the tool you are working with and the object you have selected. The default position for this palette is docked below the Menu bar.

1 To convert the Control palette into a floating palette, position your cursor on the gripper bar in the extreme left of the palette. Drag the palette gripper bar into the InDesign window; then release. Alternatively, choose Float from the Control palette menu (▶).

2 To dock the Control palette back at the top of the window, drag the palette gripper bar to a position immediately below the Menu bar, and release the mouse button. Alternatively, choose Dock at Top from the Control palette menu. You can also use the palette menu to dock the palette at the bottom of your InDesign window.

The Control palette menu button (▶) is located to the far right of the Control palette.

3 The options available in the control palette change according to the tool you are working with and the type of object(s) you have selected. All the options available in the palette are also available in other palettes or dialog boxes.

Graphic or Shape frame selected with the Selection tool

When you are working in a text frame with the Type tool selected, you can choose between the Character Formatting Controls button and the Paragraph Formatting Controls button as required:

Text frame selected with the Selection tool

Text frame with Type tool selected

Managing Palettes

A considerable amount of InDesign's functionality is accessed through palettes: you can work with floating palettes or with palettes docked into the Palette bar that runs down the extreme right edge of the InDesign window. Floating or docked palettes always appear in front of the document pages. The majority of the palettes are organized initially into combined groups, but you can create your own groupings if necessary. The following techniques will help you customize the way you work with palettes.

All palettes can be found in the Window menu. The Type menu also allows you to display palettes for Character, Paragraph, Character Styles, Paragraph Styles, Tabs and Story. When you choose a palette, it displays along with any other palettes currently in its group.

The palette menu button (▶) can be accessed whether the palette is expanded or collapsed.

Click on a palette tab in the Palette bar on the extreme right of the InDesign window to display the palette. The palette remains anchored to the Palette bar. Click on the same palette tab to collapse the palette back into the Palette bar.

Choose Window> Workspace> Save Workspace to save the current position of the palettes. Enter a name for this workspace arrangement in the Save Workspace dialog box. To reset palettes to this arrangement choose Window>Workspace, and then select the name of the workspace. Choose Default from the sub-menu to return palettes to their original positions.

To move a floating palette, position your cursor in the title bar of the palette; then press and drag. To close a floating palette, click once on the Close button in the title bar of the palette.

To make a palette active, click its tab. The tab is highlighted and the appropriate options for the palette are displayed.

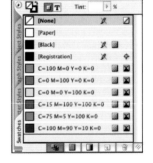

...cont'd

Managing palettes is an integral part of using InDesign. Learning to manage and work efficiently with palettes means that you will quickly begin to work confidently and productively with the software.

Some palettes (e.g. Character, Paragraph, Stroke, Align) have options that can be either hidden or made visible. Choose Show Options from the palette's pop-up menu ( ) to display a full range of options for the palette (or click the Expand/Collapse button in the palette's tab if the palette is a floating palette):

Some of the palettes (such as Swatches, Pages, Layers and Navigator) can be resized by dragging the resize icon in the bottom-right corner of the palette:

5 Drag the palette tab name out of a palette group to create a stand-alone palette. Drag a palette name tab into another palette group or individual palette to create a new custom palette. When combining palettes, release the mouse button when the palette you are dragging into becomes highlighted. You can also drag the tab of a floating palette into one of the Palette bar stations to dock it into the Palette bar.

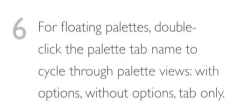

6 For floating palettes, double-click the palette tab name to cycle through palette views: with options, without options, tab only.

7 Click once on the Maximize button (Windows) or Zoom button (Mac) to completely collapse a palette. Click the same button to restore the palette to its previous state. You can also double-click a palette's title bar to completely collapse it, or to restore it to its previous state.

8 Floating palettes (such as Align, Transform, Character, Paragraph and Links) have a palette menu button (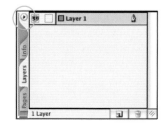) in the top-right corner, for accessing a range of commands relevant to the palette. Palettes docked in the Palette bar have a palette menu button in the top-left of the palette.

Ruler Guides

Ruler guides are non-printing guides that are used to align objects accurately. The default color for ruler guides is light blue. When Snap to Guides is on, drawing tool cursors snap onto guides when they come within four screen pixels of the guide. Also, when you move an object, the edges of the object will snap onto guides.

1. To create a ruler guide, make sure the rulers are showing; choose View>Show Rulers (Ctrl/Command + R) if they are not. Position your cursor in either the top or the left ruler; then press and drag onto the page. When you release, you create a ruler guide at that point. Look at the Control palette or the Transform palette X/Y fields

   to get a readout indicating the position of the cursor as you press and drag.

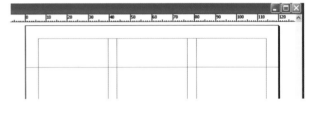

2. To create a ruler guide that runs across both pages in a spread, double-click in the ruler at the point at which you want the guide. Alternatively, drag from a ruler but release the mouse when the cursor is on the pasteboard area surrounding the page.

3. To reposition a ruler guide, select the Selection tool, position your cursor

To create a vertical and horizontal guide simultaneously, position your cursor in the crosshair area, where the vertical and horizontal rulers meet. Hold down Ctrl/Command, then press and drag onto the page. Release the mouse button before you release the Ctrl/Command key, otherwise you will reposition the Zero point:

In a document with multiple layers, ruler guides appear on the active layer. When you hide the layer you also hide the layer's ruler guides. (See page 105, Understanding Layers.)

To lock an individual guide, click on it with the Selection tool to select it. The guide changes color to indicate that it is selected. Then choose Object>Lock Position (Ctrl/Command+L). If you try to move the guide, a padlock icon appears indicating the guide's locked status. To unlock a locked guide, click on it to select it; then choose Object>Unlock Position (Ctrl/Command+Alt/option+L).

on an existing guide; then press and drag. A double-headed arrow cursor appears, indicating that you have picked up the guide.

4 To remove a ruler guide, select the Selection tool and then click on the guide. It changes color, indicating that it is selected. Press the Backspace or Delete key. Alternatively, drag the guide back into the ruler it came from.

5 To position a guide with complete precision, drag in a guide and position it roughly where you want it. Click on the guide with the Selection tool; then enter the position you want in the X or Y entry field in the Control palette or the Transform palette. Press Enter/Return to apply the new value.

6 To lock all the guides for the entire document, choose View>Lock Guides (Ctrl/Command+Alt/option+ ;). A tick mark next to the option in the menu indicates that guides are locked. Use the same option to unlock guides. The Lock Guides command also locks Margin and Column guides.

7 To hide/show all ruler guides as well as margin and column guides, choose View>Hide/Show Guides (Ctrl/Command+ ;). This command does not hide frame edge guides, which define the size and position of frames on a page. Choose View>Hide/Show Frame Edges (Ctrl/Command+H) to hide/show frame edges.

Saving Documents

You can also use the Save As command when you want to create a new version of the document on which you are working. Use File>Save As, specify a different location and/or enter a different name for the file. When you OK the Save As dialog box you continue to work on the new file; the original remains as it was when you last saved it.

It is important to be able to use the Save As, Save and Save a Copy commands as necessary.

Save	Ctrl+S
Save As...	Shift+Ctrl+S
Save a Copy...	Alt+Ctrl+S

Save As

Use the Save As command soon after starting a new document, or after converting a QuarkXPress or PageMaker file. Save As enables you to specify a folder and name for the document.

1. To save a file for the first time, choose File>Save As (Ctrl/Command +Shift+S). Use standard Windows/Mac dialog boxes to specify the folder into which you want to save the document.

Use the shortcut Ctrl/ Command+ Alt/ option+Shift+S to save all open documents at the same time.

2. Make sure the File Name entry field is highlighted. Enter a name for the document.

   Leave the Save As Type pop-up (Windows), or Format pop-up (Mac), set to InDesign CS2 Document. Click on Save. The name of the document appears in the Title bar of the InDesign window.

Save

Use the Save command regularly as you build your InDesign document, so that changes you make are not accidentally lost due to any system or power failure. Each time you use the Save

Choose File>Close when you finish working on a document. If you have not already saved the file, in the warning box that appears, click Save to save and close the file, click Cancel to return to the document without saving, or click Don't Save to close the document without saving any changes.

command, changes you have made to the document are added to the already saved version of the file. You do not need to rename the file or specify its location every time you use the Save command.

To save a file, choose File>Save (Ctrl/Command+S) at regular intervals as you build your document.

Save A Copy

Use the Save a Copy command to save a copy of the document at its present state. When you have saved a copy, you continue to work on the original file, not the copy.

To save a copy of a document at its present state, choose File>Save a Copy. Use standard Windows/Mac dialog boxes to specify the folder into which you want to save the document. Make sure the File Name entry field is highlighted. Enter a name for the document. Click the Save button. The copy is saved in the location and with the name specified. You continue to work on the original file.

Saving Templates

Save a document as a template when you want to create a series of documents with consistent layout, text formatting, color and graphic elements. For example, if you are creating a monthly newsletter, set up an InDesign document that contains all of the standard guides, master pages, style sheets, colors, placeholder frames and graphics. Each time you begin a new issue, open the template and import new content into the existing structure; this will ensure consistency from month to month.

To save a document as a template, follow the steps for the Save As command, but choose InDesign CS2 template from the Save as Type pop-up (Windows) / the Format pop-up (Mac).

InDesign CS2 document
InDesign CS2 template

Format: ✓ InDesign CS2 document
InDesign CS2 template

Zooming and Scrolling

Use the Zoom tool (Z), the Hand tool (H), the Navigator palette and the scroll bars for zooming and moving around the document.

1 Choose Window>Object & Layout>Navigator to show the Navigator palette. Double-click the zoom % entry field to highlight the existing value. Enter a new value (5-4000%); then press Return/Enter to apply it. Alternatively, drag the zoom slider to the right or left to zoom in and out. You can also click the small/large mountain buttons to change the zoom in increments.

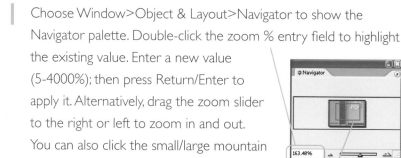

2 As you change the zoom level, the size of the red View box updates to indicate the area of the document that you have zoomed to. Position your cursor in the View box; then drag it to move quickly to other parts of the page at the same zoom level.

3 To use the Zoom tool, select it, position the zoom cursor in the document window, and then click to zoom in at the cursor position by preset increments. With the Zoom tool selected, hold down Alt/option to change the cursor to the zoom out cursor. Click to zoom out by preset decrements.

4 One powerful zoom technique is to press and drag with the Zoom tool to define an area on which you want to zoom. A dotted rectangle appears, defining the zoom area. The smaller the zoom area you define, the greater the resulting magnification.

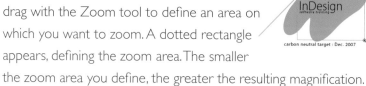

5 You can use standard scroll bar techniques to see different parts of a page, or you can use the Hand tool: select the Hand tool, position your cursor on the page, and then press and drag to scroll the page.

Undoing Mistakes

Perhaps the most essential technique when you are learning a software application is that of undoing any mistakes you make. Use the Undo command in Adobe InDesign when you make a mistake.

The number of undos you can perform is restricted only by the amount of memory (RAM) in your system.

1   To correct a mistake, choose Edit>Undo (Ctrl/Command+Z). The Undo command is dimmed if you cannot undo an operation.

Although the keyboard shortcuts for Undo/Redo are extremely convenient, using the menu option can be a useful option when you want to know exactly what step you are undoing. When you use the menu option, the wording of the Undo/Redo commands changes to indicate the step you are about to undo/redo.

2   Choose Edit>Redo (Ctrl/Command+Shift+Z) to reverse through any undos.

3   To revert to the last saved version of a file, choose File>Revert. Confirm the revert in the warning dialog box. The file reverts to the stage it was at when you last used the Save command. This option can sometimes be more efficient than using repeated Undo commands.

Margin and Column Guides

You can use the Margin and Column Guides dialog box to change margin and column settings for the currently selected master page, spread or page. A selected page or spread is indicated by a highlighted page icon in the Pages palette.

22-23

A "spread" usually consists of two pages – a left- and a right-hand page – viewed side by side. For example, when you read a magazine or a book, you are viewing spreads.

1 To change margin and/or column settings, select the page, spread or master page/spread for which you want to make changes.

2 Choose Layout> Margins and Columns. Enter new margin values.

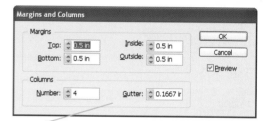

There is a difference between a 'targeted' page or spread and a 'selected' page or spread. (See page 140 for further information.)

3 Enter the number of columns and the gutter value (space between columns) for the columns. OK the dialog box.

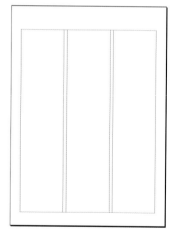

If you make changes to margin and column settings on individual pages/spreads, and then make changes to margin and column settings on the master page on which the document pages are based, the master page changes do not override the changes already made to individual pages/spreads. To reapply master page margin and column settings to a page, drag the master page icon onto the individual page icon. Release the mouse when you see the black highlight border on the page icon. It is best to do this before you have placed contents on the pages/spreads.

4 To create unequal columns, position your cursor on one of the column guides, and drag it to a new position. Both column guides move, maintaining the gutter width. You cannot move a column guide past another column guide or the edge of the page.

5 To Hide/Show margin and column guides, choose View>Hide/ Show Guides (Ctrl/Command+ ;). This command does not hide frame edge guides (which define the size and position of frames on a page). Choose View>Hide/Show Frame Edges (Ctrl/ Command+H) to hide/show frame edges.

Building Pages

Text and graphic frames, lines and basic shapes such as circles and rectangles form the fundamental building blocks of InDesign publications. This chapter shows you how to create these basic objects and then manipulate and control them to achieve the exact page layout structure you require.

Covers

Chapter Two

Creating Frames

Use the Frame tools to create containers, which define areas on your page that will hold text or images. You can construct the basic layout of a page using frames before you bring in text and import images.

There are three sets of tools you can use to create frames. The Rectangle Frame, Ellipse Frame and Polygon Frame tools create graphic frames into which you can place images. The Rectangle, Ellipse and Polygon tools allow you to create shape frames; you can change the color and stroke width. You can use the Type tool to create text frames into which you can type or import text.

Empty text frames display in- and out-ports at the upper left and lower right corners, respectively, when selected with the Selection tool. Empty graphic frames display an X running through the middle (provided that View>Show Frame Edges is selected). Empty shape frames initially have a default 1 point black stroke and no fill.

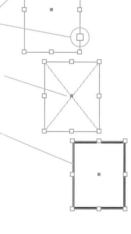

To draw a frame, select the appropriate tool; the cursor changes to the drawing tool cursor. Press and drag away from the start point, and release when the frame is the size you want. Don't worry if you don't get the shape exactly right to begin with – you can always resize and reposition the frame at a later stage.

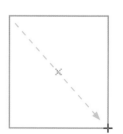

...cont'd

Choose View>Hide Frame Edges (Ctrl/ Command+H) to hide the default blue lines that define the size and shape of a frame. Frame edges are visual, on-screen guides. They do not print, but are helpful as you build a layout.

The Button tool allows you to add interactivity to a document exported as a PDF. Use standard drawing techniques to create a button frame; you can then enter text or place an image into the button:

Choose Object>Interactive> Button Options to set visibility properties, states and behaviours before you export the document as a PDF.

Select an empty text, graphic or shape frame; then choose Object>Content to access the frame type submenu. Choose from Graphic, Text or Unassigned to convert the frame to a different type:

2 When you release the mouse button, the shape is "selected" – it appears in a "bounding box" which has eight selection handles around the outside. The selection bounding box disappears when you deselect the object. A basic shape frame takes on any fill and/or stroke attributes currently set in the Toolbox. (See page 120 for information on working with fill and stroke.) Unlike basic shapes, a graphic frame does not take on any fill and/or stroke attributes currently set in the Toolbox. By default, graphic frames are ready to hold an imported image or graphic.

3 To draw a square or circular frame hold down the Shift key, and then press and drag away from the start point. The Shift key acts as a constraint on the drawing tool. Make sure you release the mouse button before the Shift key, otherwise the constraint is lost. You can also use the Shift key with the Polygon tool to maintain its proportions.

4 To draw a frame from the center out, hold down the Alt/option key before you start to drag to create the frame.

5 After you draw an object, you can continue to draw further objects, because the drawing tool remains selected. Make sure you choose the Selection tool if you want to make changes to the size or position of the object.

6 To delete a frame, select it with the Selection tool and then press the Backspace or Delete key on your keyboard.

Polygon Tools

You can use the Polygon Frame tool and the Polygon tool to draw regular polygons or stars. Use the Polygon Settings dialog box to specify the number of sides for a polygon, or the number of points for a star.

A polygon frame can hold a picture or text. A polygon shape is an object that can be filled and/or stroked with a color.

1 To draw a regular polygon, select the Polygon Frame tool or the Polygon tool, position your cursor on the page, and then press and drag to define the size of the polygon. When you release the mouse button, the polygon appears in a "bounding box" with eight selection handles around the outside. A polygon you draw with the Polygon tool takes on the Fill and Stroke attributes currently set in the Toolbox. A polygon you draw with the Polygon Frame tool has a fill and stroke of None. Hold down the Shift key as you draw with the Polygon tool to constrain the shape proportionally.

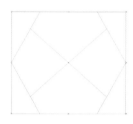

A Star Inset value of zero creates a polygon.

2 To specify the number of sides in a Polygon, double-click the Polygon tool or Polygon Frame tool. Enter a value for Number of Sides, OK the dialog box, and then press and drag to create the shape.

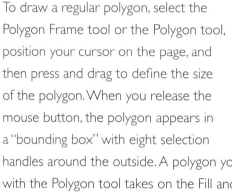

For any drawing tool, provided that View>Snap to Guides is selected, the drawing tool cursor snaps or locks onto a guide when it comes within four screen pixels of a column, margin or ruler guide. For graphic and shape frame tools, the cursor displays a hollow arrow head to indicate when it is snapping to a guide. Snap to Guides is useful when you need to create and position objects with precision.

3 To create a star, double-click the Polygon tool. Enter a value for the Number of Sides and set a value for Star Inset (0-100). The higher the value, the more "pointy" the resulting star. OK the dialog box, and then press and drag to create the shape.

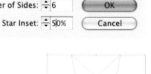

Moving Objects

You can move objects anywhere you want on the pages of your document or onto the pasteboard area surrounding your pages. Objects can cross over margins, and you can create a "bleed" by positioning an object so that it runs across the edge of a page onto the pasteboard.

1. To move or reposition an object, select the Selection tool, position your cursor inside the object, and then press and drag to move the object to a new location. If you press and drag in one swift movement, you see a blue bounding box representing the size of the object as it moves. If you press the mouse button, but pause briefly before you drag, you see a complete preview of the object as you reposition it.

2. To constrain the movement to vertical, horizontal or increments of 45 degrees, hold down Shift and then press and drag to reposition the object. Remember to release the mouse button before you release the Shift key, otherwise the constraining effect of the Shift key is lost.

3. To move an object in increments, make sure that the object is selected, and then press the up, down, left and right arrow keys on the keyboard. Each time you press an arrow key the object moves 0.0098 in. To change the amount that each press of an arrow key moves an object, choose Edit>Preferences>Units & Increments (Windows), or InDesign>Preferences>Units & Increments (Mac). Enter a new value in the Cursor Key entry field. Hold down Shift while pressing an arrow key to move an object 10 times the Cursor Key setting.

Selection Techniques

A fundamental technique in any page layout application is that of selecting objects before you make changes to them. In Adobe InDesign, you use the Selection tool to select and deselect objects.

An object in InDesign is any shape created with one of the basic shape drawing tools, any frame created with one of the frame tools, a line created with the Line tool, or any path created with the Pen or Pencil tool. Objects are the fundamental building blocks of all InDesign documents.

1 Make sure you have the Selection tool selected. Click on an object to select it. With the exception of horizontal or vertical lines, a blue bounding box with eight selection handles appears around the object, indicating that it is selected. A selection bounding box represents the horizontal and vertical dimensions of an object. The eight selection handles allow you to change the width and/or height of the object. Vertical/Horizontal lines have selection handles at both ends.

If a shape frame does not have a fill you can select it only by clicking on its path (the edge) – it is not selected if you click inside the shape.

2 To deselect one or more objects, click into some empty space with the Selection tool, or choose Edit>Deselect All (Ctrl/ Command+Shift+A).

| Select All | Ctrl+A |
| Deselect All | Shift+Ctrl+A |

3 To select more than one object, click on the first object to select it, hold down the Shift key, and then click on additional objects to add them to the selection. Multiple objects selected in this manner form a temporary grouping. For example, if you move one of the objects, the other selected objects move, maintaining the relative position of each object.

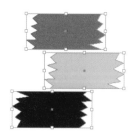

The Selection tool is used to select, resize and move objects or groups. The Direct Selection tool is used to edit the shape of paths or frames by working directly on the anchor points that form the shape. The Direct Selection tool is also used for working on the contents of graphic frames.

4 Alternatively, with the Selection tool selected, position your cursor so that it is not touching any object on the page. Press and drag; as you do so a dotted marquee box appears. Any object that this marquee touches will be selected when you release the mouse button. This is a very powerful selection technique, and it is worth practising it a few times to become familiar with it.

The Select All command does not select objects on locked or hidden layers.

5 With any tool selected you can choose Edit>Select All (Ctrl/Command+A) to select all objects on the currently active page or spread, as well as on the pasteboard area surrounding the page.

6 The Select sub-menu provides useful controls for selecting objects in complex areas of overlapping objects. Select an object, and choose Edit>Select to access the options in the sub-menu. (See page 102 for further information on changing the stacking order of objects.)

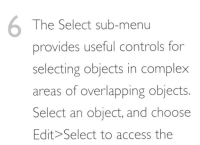

First Object Above	Alt+Shift+Ctrl+]
Next Object Above	Alt+Ctrl+]
Next Object Below	Alt+Ctrl+[
Last Object Below	Alt+Shift+Ctrl+[

The Control and Transform Palettes

The appearance of the Control palette changes when you work in a text frame with the Type tool selected. See Chapters 4 and 5 for information on using the Control palette to format type.

When you need to manipulate an object with numerical accuracy you can use the Control palette or the Transform palette. When you select an object with the Selection tool, these palettes display a range of controls for manipulating it.

The matrix of small squares to the left of the palettes are the reference points. Each point refers to a corresponding handle on the bounding box of the object. There is also a reference point for the center of the object. Click on a reference point to specify the point around which the transformation takes place.

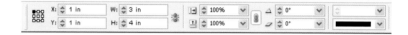

The default zero point for a page is the top left corner. Step 1 assumes that the default zero point has not been changed.

1   The X and Y entry fields allow you to position an object precisely. The X value specifies the position of the object's reference point from the left edge of the page or spread. The Y value specifies the position of the object's reference point from the top of the page.

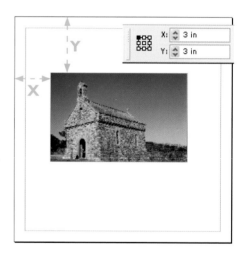

A Constrain Proportions button is selected when it appears as an unbroken chain in a white box. It appears as a broken chain when it is deselected. It is important that you can distinguish between the two states. Click the button to toggle between states:

2   To change the dimensions of an object, enter precise values in the W/H entry fields. Provided that the Constrain Proportions icon is selected, when you change either the Width or Height value, the other value updates automatically to scale the object in proportion. Changing

the Width or Height values for a graphic frame that contains an image also scales the contents of the frame (i.e. the image itself). Changing the Width or Height values for a text frame does not change the size of the type within the frame.

Select an object before you make any changes to the fields in the Control or Transform palettes, otherwise nothing will happen.

3 To scale a frame and its contents (picture or text) as a percentage, enter a scale value in the percentage entry fields, or use the pop-up to choose a preset value. To scale the width, use the Scale X Percentage field; to scale the height use the Scale Y Percentage field. Provided that the Constrain Proportions icon is selected, when you change either the Width or Height value, the other value updates automatically to scale the object in proportion.

You can also use the Rotate tool to rotate selected objects or frames manually.

4 To rotate an object, enter a value in the Rotate entry field, or use the pop-up to choose from the preset list. You can enter a positive or negative number from 0 to 360 degrees.

5 To shear an object, enter a value in the Shear entry field, or use the pop-up to choose from the preset list.

Press Enter/ Return to apply any new value you enter in the Control or Transform palette.

6 To apply a stroke to an object, click into the Stroke Weight field and then enter a value, or choose a value from the Stroke Weight list. Choose a style for the stroke from the Stroke Type list.

The Measure tool (K), in conjunction with the Info palette, is useful when you need to measure the distance from one object to another. Select the Measure tool; then drag from one point to another. When you release the mouse button, the measure line appears on your screen. A readout of the distance appears in the Info palette:

Select the Selection tool to hide the measure line.

7 When you select a graphic frame that contains an image, the Control palette displays a set of additional options. Click the Select Container or Select Content button to toggle the selection status between the frame and the image inside. Use the Fitting options to control how the image fits inside the frame dimensions. (See page 89 for further information on working with images and graphic frames.) When you are working with a group, use the Select Next/Previous Object in Group buttons to select through the objects in the group.

The Transform Palette

The Transform palette is a convenient floating palette that provides a range of controls similar to, but less comprehensive than, those in the Control palette. Choose Window>Transform (F9) to show the palette if it is not already showing.

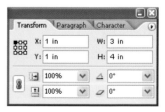

Lines

Choose Window> Stroke (F10) to show the Stroke palette if it is not already showing.

Use the Line tool to create horizontal and vertical lines, or lines at any angle. You can modify lines using the Selection tools or using the Control or Transform palettes. Use the Stroke palette to change line weight, to add arrow heads, and to create dashed or dotted lines.

1   To draw a horizontal or vertical line, select the Line tool (\ ). Position your cursor on the page, hold down the Shift key, and then press and drag. Release the mouse button before the Shift key when the line is the desired length. The line remains selected when you release, indicated by the two selection handles.

Press F9 to show the Transform palette if it is not already showing.

2   To edit a horizontal or vertical line, select the Selection tool, click on the line to select it, and drag one of the end points. The vertical/horizontal constraint remains in effect as you resize the line.

To convert a horizontal or vertical line to an angled line, select it with the Direct Selection tool and then drag one of the end anchor points:

3   To draw a line at any angle across your page, select the Line tool, position your cursor on the page, and then press and drag. When you release, the line remains selected, indicated by a selection bounding box with eight selection handles.

4   To edit a line at any angle, select the Selection tool and then click the line to select it. The bounding box appears around the line. Drag any of the selection handles to change the start or end point of the line. Alternatively, select the line with the Direct Selection tool. Drag an end point to resize the line.

5   To change the thickness of a selected line, choose Window>Stroke (or click the Stroke tab in the Palette bar) to show the Stroke palette if it is not already showing. To change the

thickness of the line, you can click the Weight increment buttons to change the thickness in single point increments, enter an exact value in the Weight entry box and press Enter/Return, or choose a setting from the Weight pop-up list.

Lines and the Control palette

You can use the Control palette to control line attributes with numeric precision.

See pages 36–37 for further details on using the Control palette.

1 Use the Selection tool to select the line you want to change. Click on the start, end or midpoint reference point for the line, to specify the point on the line to which changes refer.

See page 36 for information on working with coordinates.

2 Enter values in the X and Y entry fields to specify the exact position for the chosen reference point of the line.

3 Enter a value in the L entry field to specify the length of the line. Alternatively, use the Scale X Percentage and the Scale Y Percentage to change the length of the line; Scale X and Scale Y have the same effect on a line, provided that the Constrain Proportions for scaling button is selected.

You can use the Transform palette to change line attributes with numeric precision. Choose Window>Transform (F9) to show the palette if it is not already showing. The controls available in the palette offer a convenient subset of those in the Control palette.

4 Use the Rotate and Shear entry fields to rotate and shear the line. Shearing on a line becomes apparent when you increase its Stroke weight. (See page 37 for further information on rotating and shearing objects.)

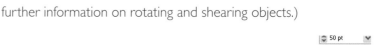

5 Choose a style for the line from the Style pop-up list.

Manually Resizing Objects

Once you've drawn an object you can resize it manually using the Selection tool. You can resize basic objects, open paths, graphic and text frames and groups.

To maintain the proportions of an object as you resize it, hold down Shift as you drag a selection handle.

For basic shapes and paths, if you press and drag on a selection handle in one movement, you see a blue bounding box that represents the new size of the object. If you press on the selection handle, pause momentarily, and then drag, you see a representation of the complete shape as you resize it:

When you use this technique on an object with Text Wrap applied to it, you see a live preview of text reflowing as you change the size of the object.

1 To resize a basic shape or frame, select the Selection tool. Click on the object (or group); the object is highlighted and eight selection handles appear around the outside. An irregularly shaped object appears within a blue rectangular bounding box with handles.

2 Drag the centre left/right handle to increase/decrease only the width of the object. Drag the center top/bottom handle to resize only the height. Drag a corner handle to resize width and height simultaneously.

3 To maintain the proportions of an object or group, hold down Shift and drag a selection handle.

4 To resize a line drawn at an angle, select it using the Selection tool. Notice that dragging a handle changes the start or end position of the line, in effect changing the length of the line. To change the thickness of a line use the Stroke palette. (See pages 39–40 for further information on using the Stroke palette.)

5 When you manually resize an object using the Selection tool, the Stroke weight remains constant.

Cut, Copy, Paste, Clear

The Clipboard provides one of the most convenient and flexible methods for copying, cutting and pasting objects, frames, groups and text. The limitation of the clipboard is that it holds the result of only one cut or copy command at a time. As soon as you perform another cut or copy, the newly cut or copied object replaces the previous contents of the clipboard.

1 Use the Selection tool to select an object, frame or group; then choose Edit>Cut/Copy. Copy leaves the original on the page and places a copy of the selected object onto the clipboard. Cut removes the selected object from the page and places it on the clipboard.

Cut	Ctrl+X
Copy	Ctrl+C
Paste	Ctrl+V
Paste without Formatting	Shift+Ctrl+V
Paste Into	Alt+Ctrl+V
Paste in Place	Alt+Shift+Ctrl+V
Clear	Backspace

2 Highlight a range of text using the Type tool and then choose Edit>Cut/Copy to place selected text onto the clipboard. (See page 50, Chapter 3, for further information on copying and pasting text.)

3 To paste objects and frames that have been copied to the clipboard back into a document, make sure the Selection tool is selected, and choose Edit>Paste (Ctrl/Command+V). The contents of the clipboard are pasted into the center of your screen display.

4 Choose Edit>Clear (Ctrl/Command+Backspace) for a selected object, frame or group to delete the selected object(s) from the document completely. The clear command does not use the clipboard and therefore does not affect its contents.

5 Choose Edit>Paste in Place (Ctrl/Command+Alt/option+Shift+V) to paste an object or group onto a page in exactly the same position as that from which it was cut.

Text Basics

This chapter covers essential techniques, such as importing text, highlighting text, basic text editing techniques and threading or linking text frames. It is important to master these everyday routines and procedures.

Covers

Chapter Three

Entering and Importing Text

When you draw a text frame, the Type tool draws from the baseline indicator, the bar that crosses the I-beam about three quarters of the way down the cursor, not from the top of the cursor:

There is a range of techniques for entering text into an InDesign document. You can enter text directly into a text frame using the keyboard, paste text already stored on the clipboard into a text frame, or import a text file prepared in a wide variety of wordprocessing applications into a text frame or directly into the InDesign document. Remember, when you type, paste or import text, it appears at the Text insertion point.

1 To create a text frame, select the Type tool. Position your cursor on the page; then press and drag. This defines the size and position of your text frame. When you release, you will see a Text insertion point flashing in the top-left corner of the frame.

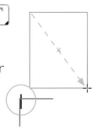

You cannot position the Type tool cursor inside an existing text frame to draw another frame. This can sometimes cause a slight confusion, particularly when there is a large, empty text frame on your page and frame edges are not showing – in which case, it is not immediately obvious why you cannot draw the new text frame.

2 To enter text directly into the frame, begin typing on the keyboard. Text wraps automatically when it reaches the right edge of the text frame. Press Enter/Return only when you want to begin a new paragraph. By default, text is formatted as Times Roman 12pt.

Begin typing on the keyboard to enter text in the text frame.

3 To import a wordprocessed file, make sure you have a text frame, a graphic frame or a basic shape selected. You need not select the Type tool. Choose File>Place. Use standard Windows/Mac dialog boxes to locate the text file

You can drag a text file directly from Windows Explorer or Macintosh Finder into the InDesign document window. The text is added in a new text frame.

you want to place. Click on its name to select it. If you want to make sure that typographer's quotes (rather than foot and inch symbols) are used in the imported text, or if you want to remove

If the text file you import contains more text than will fit into the text frame, the overflow marker appears near the bottom right corner of the frame to indicate that there is overmatter.

Taken together, all these statistics point to the increasing importance, visibility and complexity of supply chain management in today's chemical industry. If the talks succeeded, the green one, depicting a restructured, lower-cost network carrier, would to be released. After two months of jockeying, neither side has budged. The court overseeing the restructuring has ordered negotia-

You can make the frame bigger, or the text smaller, or you can thread the text into another frame (see page 51) to make the remaining text visible.

formatting already applied in the Word file, then select Show Import Options. When you click Open, a secondary import options dialog box appears. Select the Use Typographer's Quotes option to ensure that straight quotes and apostrophes are converted into typographic

equivalents. Select the Remove Styles and Formatting from Text and Tables radio button to discard Word formatting.

4 Click the OK button. Graphic frames and basic shapes are converted automatically into text frames, and the text flows in.

Mapping Word Styles

The Microsoft Word Import Options dialog box allows you to map styles from a Word document to Paragraph Styles in InDesign.

To place text without first creating a text frame, use the Place command to locate the text file you want to place. After you select a file and click Open, the cursor changes to the Loaded text cursor:

Position the cursor, then click to place the text into a default-width text frame. If you click within column guides, InDesign creates a text frame to the width of the guides. Alternatively, press and drag with the Loaded text cursor to define the width and height of the text frame into which the text will flow.

1 In the Import Options dialog box, select the Preserve Styles and Formatting from Text and Tables radio button. Select the Customize Style Import radio button and then click Style Mapping.

2 In the Style Mapping dialog box, select a Word style; then select the InDesign paragraph style you want to map it to from the pop-up menu that appears in the InDesign Style column. Click OK.

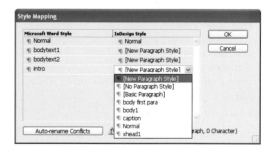

Basic Text Editing

Almost as soon as you start working with text you will need to be able to make changes and corrections – correcting spelling errors, changing punctuation, deleting words and so on. Use the Type tool to make changes to text.

1 To make an alteration to your text, select the Type tool. Click in the text frame where you want to make changes. The text frame does not have to be selected before you click into it; if the frame is selected, the selection handles on the frame disappear. A Text insertion point appears at the exact point at which you click. The Text insertion point is the point at which text will appear if you type it on the keyboard, paste it from the clipboard, or import it using the Place command.

Once upon a time, there was a poor hunter. One day he came across|a trapped crane. He took pity on the crane and released it. A few days later, a lovely woman visited his house, and asked him to shelter her for the night.

If you are working with the Selection tool, you can double-click on a text frame to quickly select the Type tool and place the Text insertion point where you click.

2 Notice that when you move your cursor within an active text box, it becomes the I-beam cursor. Position the I-beam cursor anywhere in the text and click to reposition the Text insertion point.

To show/hide invisible text characters such as spaces, tabs and carriage return markers, choose Type>Show/Hide Hidden Characters. In InDesign, the hashmark symbol (#) represents the end of the text file:

My beautiful fish¶
My fish shines in the deep blue ocean waves.¶
    » My fish shines and shimmers when happy. My fish glows and sparkles when it plays games with his friends.#

3 To move the Text insertion point character by character through the text, press the left or right arrow key on the keyboard. To move the cursor up or down one line at a time, press the up or down arrow key.

4 To delete one character to the left of the Text insertion point, press the Backspace key. To delete one character to the right of the Text insertion point, press the Delete key.

Highlighting Text

Use the following techniques to highlight text before you make changes. For example, once you have highlighted text you can delete, overtype, cut or copy it. Highlighting text is also a crucial step before you change its formatting. Use the Type tool to select text.

You sometimes need to zoom in on text in order to highlight the exact characters you want.

1 Position the type cursor at the start of the text you want to highlight. Press and drag across the text. As you do so the text will "reverse out" to indicate exactly what is selected. Drag the cursor, horizontally, vertically or diagonally across the text,

Once upon a time, there was a poor hunter. One day he came across a trapped crane. He took pity on the crane and released it. A few days later, a lovely woman visited his house, and asked him to shelter her from

the stor
More tl
suffer b
done to
more in
sae plus
Nationa

depending on the range of text you want to highlight. Using this technique, you must select all the text you want to select with one movement of the mouse. You can't release and then drag again to add to the original selection. This is a very important technique. Practice it a number of times to become familiar with it. Use this technique to select any amount of visible text.

When you have selected a range of text, if you press any key on the keyboard you are overtyping the selected text. Whatever you type replaces the selected text. If this happens unintentionally, choose Edit>Undo Typing immediately.

2 Position your cursor on a word, and double-click to highlight one word. This is useful when you want to delete a complete word, or when you want to replace the word with another word by overtyping it.

My beautiful fish
My fish shines in the deep blue ocean waves. My fish shines and shimmers

My beautiful fish
My fish shines in the deep blue ocean waves. My fish shines and shimmers when happy. My fish glows and sparkles when it plays games with his friends. My fish bubbles playfully when he talks. My fish loves the coral reef when he swims past.
My fish sparkles like a rainbow in the sky on a rainy day. My fish is very proud of his scales.

3 Click three times in a paragraph to select the entire paragraph.

4 Position your cursor at the start of the text you want to highlight. Click the mouse button to place the Text insertion point. This marks the start of the text you want to highlight. Move your cursor to the end of the text you want to highlight. It is important that you do not press and drag the mouse at this stage: simply find the end of the text you want to highlight.

My beautiful fish
My fish shines in the deep blue ocean waves. My fish shines and shimmers when happy. My fish glows and sparkles when it plays games with his friends. My fish bubbles playfully when he talks. My fish loves the coral reef when he swims past.
My fish sparkles like a rainbow in the sky on a rainy day. My fish is very proud of his scales.

Hold down Shift, and then click to indicate the end of the text. Text between the initial click and the Shift+click is highlighted. This is a useful technique when you want to highlight a range of text that runs across several pages.

5 Click into the text to place the Text insertion point; then choose Edit>Select All (Ctrl/Command+A) to select the entire text file, even if it is linked through multiple pages. This includes any overmatter, even though you cannot see it.

6 To deselect text, select the type tool and click anywhere within the text frame.

The Text Insertion Point

The Text Insertion Point is the thin vertical line that appears when you click into a text frame with the Type tool. It indicates the point at which text will be added if you press keys on the keyboard.

Use the following techniques for fast and efficient editing of text in your documents.

> Once upon a time, there was a poor hunter. One day he came across|a trapped crane. He took pity on the crane and released it. A few days later, a lovely woman visited his house, and asked him to shelter her for the night.

1   To move the Text insertion point one word left or right at a time, hold down Ctrl/Command and use the left/right arrow keys.

Select the Type tool and then click into an empty graphic or shape frame to convert it into a text frame.

2   To move the Text insertion point up or down one paragraph at a time, hold down Ctrl/Command and use the up/down arrow keys.

3   To move the Text insertion point to the end of a line, press the End key. To move the Text insertion point to the beginning of a line, press the Home key.

4   To move the Text insertion point to the start of the story, hold down Ctrl/Command and press the Home key. To move the Text insertion point to the end of the story, hold down Ctrl/Command and press the End key.

5   Add Shift to any of the above keyboard combinations to highlight the range of text that the Text insertion point moves across. For example, to highlight from the current Text insertion point to the end of the text file, including any overmatter, hold down Ctrl/Command+Shift and press the End key.

Cutting, Copying and Pasting Text

Use the Cut, Copy and Paste commands when you want to move words, phrases or paragraphs from one place to another in a document. You can also use these commands to copy text from one InDesign document to another.

See page 42 for information on cutting and copying objects to the clipboard.

1 To copy or cut text, first highlight a range of text. Choose Edit>Cut/Copy. The text is stored temporarily on the clipboard.

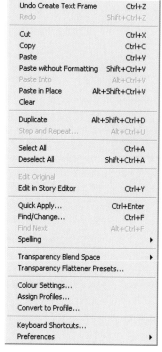

2 To paste text back into a text frame, select the Type tool; then click into a text frame to place the Text insertion point at the point at which you want to place the text.

With the Text insertion point in a text frame, you can quickly fill the entire frame with placeholder text by choosing Type>Fill with Placeholder Text. InDesign inserts meaningless Latin text to fill the frame.

3 Choose Edit>Paste.

4 If you choose Edit>Paste without first positioning the Text insertion point, a copy of the text on the clipboard is placed in a new text frame in the center of the screen display.

5 Choose Edit>Clear, or press the Backspace key on your keyboard, when you want to delete selected text without storing a copy of it on the clipboard.

Threading Text

A text frame drawn with the Type tool has empty In and Out ports, which are visible when you select the frame with the Selection tool. Graphic or Shape frames can display In and Out ports only when they have been converted to text frames (Object>Content>Text).

Threading is the technique by which you link text from one frame into another frame when there is too much text to fit in the first frame (and you don't want to make the type smaller or the frame bigger). Additional text that will not fit in a text frame is referred to as overmatter or overset text. It is indicated by a red "+" symbol in the out port, near the bottom right corner of the text frame.

You can thread text from one frame to another frame on either the same page or a different page. If necessary, threads can jump multiple pages.

Although you can thread empty text frames, it is easier to understand how threading works if you are flowing a text file.

When you click on the overset text marker, you load up the cursor with the overmatter. The shape of the Loaded text cursor changes, depending on where you place the cursor. If you place the cursor over empty space on your page or on the pasteboard it displays as the Loaded text cursor:

If you place the cursor over an empty text frame it displays as the Thread text cursor:

If you place it over an empty graphic or shape frame it becomes the Convert to text frame cursor:

1 Place a text file into a text frame. (See pages 44–45 for information on placing text files.) Make sure there is more text than will fit into the frame. A red "+" symbol appears in the Out port.

> Taken together, all these statistics point to the increasing importance, visibility and complexity of supply chain management in today's chemical industry. If the talks succeeded, the green one, depicting a restructured, lower-cost network carrier, would to be released. After two months of jockeying, neither side has budged. The court overseeing the restructuring has ordered negotiating sessions, but

2 Draw another text frame. Using the Selection tool, reselect the frame that holds the text. Click once on the "+" symbol. The cursor changes to the Loaded text cursor.

3 Position your cursor in the next text frame. The cursor changes to the Thread text cursor.

4 Click to flow text into the frame.

> Taken together, all these statistics point to the increasing importance, visibility and complexity of supply chain management in today's chemical industry. If the talks succeeded, the green one, depicting a restructured, lower-cost network carrier, would to be released. After two months of jockeying, neither side has budged. The court overseeing the restructuring has ordered negotiating sessions, but

If you place the Loaded text cursor over a text frame that contains text, and then click, the existing text is replaced with the text from the Loaded text cursor.

5 Repeat the process until there is no more text to thread. You know that there is no more text to thread when the Out port is empty.

Taken together, all these statistics point to the increasing importance, visibility and complexity of supply chain management in today's chemical industry. If the talks succeeded, the green one, depicting a restructured, lower-cost network carrier, would to be released. After two months of jockeying, neither side has budged. The court overseeing the restructuring has ordered negotiating sessions, but

refuses to impose its own solution.
Chemical companies are still failing to realise the enormous potential value in the supply chain. The decision is in line with an antidumping investigation started on 6 March last year, it said.
What sets regional carriers apart, however, has been their consistent profitably. The unions insist that when they agreed last summer to a package of labour conces-

sions worth an estimated $1.1 billion, the quid pro quo was that pensions would be left alone. We do not track where you go on our sites, so you never receive unsolicited emails from us or our advertisers. .
Chemical companies are still failing to realise the enormous potential value in the supply chain.

6 You don't have to create another text frame in order to thread text. You can simply click on the "+" symbol, position your Loaded text cursor, and then press and drag to define the next text frame. When you release the mouse button, the overset text flows into the area you define.

The Info palette provides character, word, line and paragraph count information when you are working with the Type tool in a text frame. A "+" symbol indicates amounts of overset text:

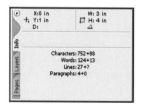

7 Alternatively, you can position your Loaded text cursor on your page, and then click to place the overset text. InDesign automatically creates a text frame to the width of the page margins, or any column guides within which you click. The frame starts where you click and ends on the bottom margin of the page.

Semi-Automatic Text Flow

Semi-automatic text flow is useful when you have a long text file that you want to thread through several existing text frames.

1 To activate semi-automatic text flow, with the Selection tool, click on an overset text marker as if linking manually. Hold down Alt/option (the cursor changes to the Semi-automatic text cursor), and click in the next frame to flow text into it. The text cursor reloads if there is more overmatter to place.

2 Keep the Alt/option key held down. Click into the next frame. Repeat the process as necessary.

Understanding Text Threads

Understanding the symbols that appear in the In and Out ports, and how to control and manipulate them, is essential for working efficiently and accurately with threaded frames. Each port is represented by a small square located on the edge of a text frame.

An empty In port in the top left corner of a text frame indicates that this is the first frame in the thread – no text flows into this frame from another frame.

Taken together, al
statistics point to
increasing import
visibility and com

A solid triangle symbol in the In port indicates that the frame is part of a threaded story – text from a preceding frame flows into it.

refuses to impose it
solution.
Chemical compani
still failing to realiz

Use the keyboard shortcut Ctrl/ Command+Alt/ option+Y to Show/Hide threads. Threads are visible provided that at least one text frame in the threaded story is selected.

A red "+" symbol in the Out port in the bottom right of a frame indicates overset text. This overset text can be linked to another frame. A solid triangle symbol in the Out port indicates that this frame is already linked to another frame.

tisers.
ical companies are
iling to realize the
ous potential value

An empty Out port indicates there is no overset text and that the frame is not linked to any other frame.

hemical companies are
ill failing to realize the
ormous potential value
the supply chain.

Text Threads

Each text thread is represented by a blue line running from an Out port to an In port.

To show text threads, choose View>Show Text Threads. Select a text frame to see the text threads, which indicate the flow of text through the threaded frames.

Taken together, all these statistics point to the increasing importance, visibility and complex- ity of supply chain management in today's chemical industry. If the talks succeeded, the green one, depicting a restructured, lower-cost network carrier, would to be released. After two months of jockeying, neither side has budged.	The court overseeing the restructuring has ordered negotiating sessions, but refuses to impose its own solution. Chemical companies are still failing to realize the enormous potential value in the supply chain. The decision is in line with an antidumping investiga- tion started on 6 March last year, it said. What sets regional car-	riers apart, however, has been their consistent profitably. The unions insist that when they agreed last summer to a package of labor conces- sions worth an estimated $1.1 billion, the quid pro quo was that pensions would be left alone. We do not track

If at any time you pick up the Loaded text cursor accidentally, you can 'unload' it, without placing or losing any text, by clicking on any other tool in the Toolbox.

Breaking Threads

In order to manage and control threaded text in a document you sometimes need to break the thread between connected frames.

1   To break the threaded link between frames, select the Selection tool, and then click into a frame in a series of threaded text frames. The In and Out ports show when you activate a series of threaded frames. Text threads appear, provided that View>Show Text Threads is selected.

You can also break a thread by clicking in the In port of a threaded text frame, and then clicking anywhere inside the same text frame.

2   Click once in the Out port of the frame where you want to break the thread. Position your cursor within the frame whose Out port you clicked. The cursor changes to the Unthread cursor.

3   Click in the frame to break the thread between the frames.

4   Instead of steps 2–3 above, you can double-click an In or Out port to break the connection between frames.

Taken together, all these statistics point to the increasing importance, visibility and complexity of supply chain management in today's chemical industry. If the talks succeeded, the green one, depicting a restructured, lower-cost network carrier, would to be released. After two months of jockeying. neither side has budged.

The court overseeing the restructuring has ordered negotiating sessions, but refuses to impose its own solution.
Chemical companies are still failing to realize the enormous potential value in the supply chain.

Taken together, all these statistics point to the increasing importance, visibility and complexity of supply chain management in today's chemical industry. If the talks succeeded, the green one, depicting a restructured, lower-cost network carrier, would to be released. After two months of jockeying. neither side has budged.

Deleting Frames

To delete a frame that is part of a threaded story, select the frame using the Selection tool, and then press the Backspace or Delete key. Text reflows through the remaining frames and no text is lost.

Story Editor

The Story Editor provides an alternative environment for editing text – it is a simple, straightforward, word processing environment that makes it easy to focus on text without any distractions caused by layout issues.

1   To move a story into the Story Editor window, select a text frame with the Selection tool, or, working with the Type tool, click into a text frame to place the Text insertion point.

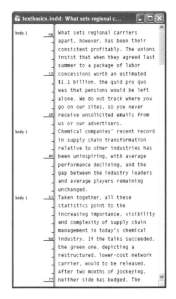

2   Choose Edit>Edit in Story Editor (Ctrl/Command+Y) to open the text in the Story Editor window. Use the same text handling and editing techniques in the Story Editor window as you do in the layout window. Changes you make to your text in Story Editor are applied immediately to the text in the layout window.

3   Choose View>Hide/Show Style Name Column to hide or show the style name column that appears on the left of the Story Editor window. Changes you make to the status of the Style name column are applied to all open Story Editor windows and any that you subsequently open.

4   To return to InDesign layout view, but leave the Story Editor window open, choose Edit>Edit in Layout. The Text insertion point appears at exactly the same position in both environments. To return to layout view and close the Story Editor window, click the Close button on the Story Editor window.

Glyphs

A Glyph is a specific instance of a character. You can use the Glyphs palette to locate additional characters that are not available on the keyboard. Open Type fonts offer glyphs that are alternative letterforms for the same character; for example, Adobe Caslon Pro has small cap and ornament variations for the letter A.

1 To insert a glyph, using the Type tool, click to place the Text insertion point in your text. Choose Type>Glyphs.

2 In the Glyphs palette, use the Font pop-up at the bottom of the palette to choose a font family. Choose a style from the Style pop-up menu next to it.

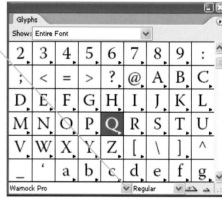

Alternative glyphs are not available in all fonts.

3 Scroll through the Glyph palette to locate the letterform you want to insert. Double-click on the glyph to insert it at the Text insertion point.

4 A small triangle on the glyph box indicates that there are alternative glyphs available. To insert an alternative glyph, press and hold the glyph to reveal the alternatives in a pop-up box. Move your cursor onto the glyph you want to insert, and then release the mouse.

Special Characters and White Space

InDesign makes it easy to insert special characters such as Em and En dashes, bullets and discretionary hyphens. You can also insert a range of different spaces to meet specific requirements. Use either the Type menu or a context-sensitive menu to access both sets of options.

A discretionary hyphen is a hyphen you use to hyphenate words manually. Unlike an ordinary hyphen, the discretionary hyphen will not appear if text reflows and the word no longer needs to be hyphenated.

Special Characters

1 To enter a special character, select the Type tool, and then click in the text at the point at which you want to insert the character.

2 Choose Type>Insert Special Character. Select the character you want to insert from the sub-menu.

The Insert Break Character sub-menu can be accessed using the same techniques as you use for the Special Character sub-menu.

3 To use the context-sensitive menu, click the right mouse button (Windows) / hold down control and click the mouse button (Mac). Choose Insert Special Character from the context-sensitive menu, and then click on the special character you want to include in the text.

Auto Page Number	Alt+Shift+Ctrl+N
Next Page Number	Alt+Shift+Ctrl+]
Previous Page Number	Alt+Shift+Ctrl+[
Section Marker	
Bullet Character	Alt+8
Copyright Symbol	Alt+G
Ellipsis	Alt+;
Paragraph Symbol	Alt+7
Registered Trademark Symbol	Alt+R
Section Symbol	Alt+6
Trademark Symbol	
Em Dash	Alt+Shift+-
En Dash	Alt+-
Discretionary Hyphen	Shift+Ctrl+-
Nonbreaking Hyphen	Alt+Ctrl+-
Double Left Quotation Mark	Alt+[
Double Right Quotation Mark	Alt+Shift+[
Single Left Quotation Mark	Alt+]
Single Right Quotation Mark	Alt+Shift+]
Tab	Tab
Right Indent Tab	Shift+Tab
Indent to Here	Ctrl+\
End Nested Style Here	

Forced line breaks are also referred to as "soft returns". They are useful when you want to turn text onto a new line without creating a new paragraph (in headlines, introductory paragraphs, subheads and the like, where it is important to control the look of your text).

The keyboard shortcut is Shift+Enter/Return.

White Space

InDesign offers a wide choice of white space options to meet specific typesetting requirements. For example, you might use a Figure space to ensure that numbers align accurately in a financial table.

Em Space	Shift+Ctrl+M
En Space	Shift+Ctrl+N
Flush Space	
Hair Space	Alt+Shift+Ctrl+I
Nonbreaking Space	Alt+Ctrl+X
Thin Space	Alt+Shift+Ctrl+M
Figure Space	
Punctuation Space	

1 To insert a space of a specific size, use the techniques described above, but choose Insert White Space from the Type or context-sensitive menu to access the White Space sub-menu options.

Text Frame Options – Columns

The Text Frame Options dialog box provides a set of important controls for working with text frames. You can divide a frame into columns and you can position type within the frames with numerical accuracy.

Columns

Dividing a single text frame into a number of columns makes it easy to create multi-column layouts and especially easy to create equal columns that do not necessarily match the number of columns in the underlying page grid – defined in the New Document dialog box.

Select the Preview option in the Text Frame Options dialog box to preview changes in the document before you click OK to accept the settings.

1 To specify columns for a text frame, select the frame and choose Object>Text Frame Options (Ctrl/Command+B).

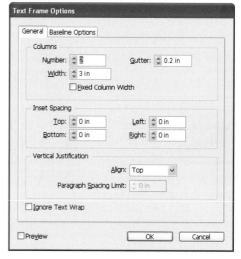

2 When you want to maintain the exact dimensions of the text frame but divide it up into equal columns, make sure that the Fixed Column Width option is deselected. Enter a value for the Number of columns. Enter a value for the Gutter – the space between columns.

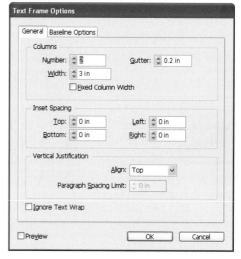

Click the Baseline Options tab in the Text Frame Options dialog box to set a custom baseline grid for the selected text frame.

Chemicals make chemistry
Taken together, all these statistics point to the increasing importance, visibility and complexity of supply chain management in today's chemical industry. If the talks succeeded, the green one, depicting a restructured, lower-cost network carrier, would to be released. After two months of jockeying, neither side has budged. The court overseeing the restructuring has ordered negotiating sessions, but refuses to impose its own solution.
Chemical companies are still failing to realize the enormous potential value in the supply chain. The decision is in line with an antidumping investigation started on 6 March last year, it said.
What sets regional carriers apart, however, has been their consistent profitably. The unions insist that when they agreed last summer to a package of labor concessions worth an estimated $1.1 billion, the quid pro quo was that pensions would be left alone. We do not track

Chemicals make chemistry
Taken together, all these statistics point to the increasing importance, visibility and complexity of supply chain management in today's chemical industry. If the talks succeeded, the green one, depicting a restructured, lower-cost network carrier, would to be released. After two months of jockeying, neither side has budged. The court overseeing the restructuring has ordered negotiating sessions, but refuses to impose its own solution. Chemical companies are still failing to realize the enormous potential value in the supply chain. The decision is in line with an antidumping investigation started on 6 March last year, it said. What sets regional carriers apart, however, has been their consistent profitably. The unions insist that when they agreed last summer to a package of labor concessions worth an estimated $1.1 billion, the quid pro quo was that pensions would be left alone. We do not track

As you change either the Number of columns or the Gutter value, the column Width field changes automatically as InDesign takes into account the size of the text frame and the Number of columns and Gutter settings. Using this procedure, the size of the text frame is not altered and you end up with equal columns within the overall frame width.

3 If you want to modify a text frame to end up with a number of columns of a specific measure or width, make sure that you select the Fixed Column Width option. Enter values for Number of columns and Gutter, and an exact value for the Width of the columns. OK the dialog box. The overall width of the text frame is adjusted according to the settings to give the exact number of columns of the specified width.

4 With Fixed Column Width selected, if you change either the Number of columns or the Gutter

Chemicals make chem-istry
Taken together, all these statistics point to the increasing importance, visibility and complexity of supply chain manage-ment in today's chemi-cal industry. If the talks succeeded, the green one, depicting a restructured, lower-cost network carrier, would to be released. After two months of jockeying,

neither side has budged. The court overseeing the restructuring has ordered negotiating sessions, but refuses to impose its own solution.
Chemical companies are still failing to realize the enormous potential value in the supply chain. The decision is in line with an antidumping investigation started on 6 March last year, it said.

What sets regional carriers apart, however, has been their consistent profitably. The unions insist that when they agreed last summer to a package of labor conces-sions worth an estimated $1.1 billion, the quid pro quo was that pensions would be left alone. We do not track

width, the width of the text frame is adjusted accordingly. Also, if you resize the width of the text frame manually, you can do so only in multiples of the column width. This ensures that you always end up with fixed-width columns.

Text Frame Insets & Vertical Alignment

Insets

Apply insets to a text frame when you have colored the background of the frame, or changed its stroke, and you want to move the text inward from the edge of the frame.

To apply text insets to a text frame, select the frame and choose Object>Text Frame Options. Enter Inset Spacing values for Top, Bottom, Left and Right. You can use the arrows to change the settings in increments. To specify a value in points, enter a value followed by "pt". When the text frame is selected, the inset is represented by a blue rectangle within the text frame. This disappears when the frame is not selected.

Vertical Alignment

The Vertical Justification option controls the position of the text vertically in the text frame. The Center option is often useful when you have a headline in a color frame.

The default Vertical Justification alignment is Top. To change the vertical alignment for text in a frame, choose Object>Text Frame Options (Ctrl/Command+B). Choose an option from the Vertical Justification Align pop-up menu.

Character Settings

Setting type is an essential discipline in creating attractive publications that are easy to read and that convey their message clearly and effectively.

Adobe InDesign has been specifically developed to offer the highest standard of typesetting it is possible to attain using current desktop computer technology. As well as offering fine control over typographic features such as type size, leading, kerning and tracking, it also provides a choice of two text composition engines, offering new opportunities for achieving high-quality typesetting from desktop computers.

Covers

Chapter Four

Font, Size, Style

Font

A font is a complete set of characters (upper case, lower case, numerals, symbols and punctuation marks) in a particular typeface, size and style. For example, 18 point Arial Bold. The term typeface describes the actual design or cut of the specific characters. Arial is a typeface, and there can be many versions of the typeface, such as Arial Narrow, Arial Black and so on.

Typefaces fall into two main categories – Serif and Sans Serif. Aldine, used in this paragraph, is an example of a serif typeface. Serifs are the small additional embellishments or strokes that end the horizontal and vertical strokes of a character. Serif faces are often used to suggest classical, established values and tradition.

Gill Sans is an example of a Sans Serif typeface. Sans Serif faces do not have the additional embellishments finishing off horizontal and vertical strokes and are often used to create a modern, contemporary look and feel.

1 To change the font for highlighted text, choose Type>Font. Select a font from the list of available fonts that appears in the sub-menu.

2 Alternatively, make sure that the Character Formatting Controls button is selected in the Control palette, and then click on the Font pop-up menu to choose from the font list.

...cont'd

To increase/ decrease the point size of selected text in 2-point increments, hold down Ctrl/ Command+Shift, and press the < or > key. The increment is set in the Units & Increments preferences dialog box. Choose Edit>Preferences>Units & Increments (Windows), or InDesign>Preferences>Units & Increments (Mac). Enter a value in the Size/Leading entry field to change the increment; an increment of 1 gives greater control and precision.

To manually resize a selected text frame and the text inside it in proportion, select the frame with the Selection tool, position your cursor on a corner handle, hold down Ctrl/Command+Shift, then drag the handle.

When you are learning InDesign, remember to make use of the tool tips, which provide explanatory labels for the icons in the Control and Character palettes. To show a tool tip, position your cursor on an icon; don't move it for a second or so and the tool tip should appear:

Size

You can enter a type size value from 0.1 to 1296 points. Type size can be entered to .01 point accuracy; for example, you can enter a value of 9.25 points.

1 Make sure you select some text. Choose Type>Size. Select a size from the preset list in the sub-menu. If you choose "Other" then the size entry field in the Character palette is highlighted. Choosing "Other" will show the Character palette if it is not already showing.

2 Alternatively, in the Control palette, either use the size pop-up to choose from the preset list, or highlight the size entry field and enter a value. Press the Enter/Return key to apply the change. You can also click the arrows ( ) to increase or decrease the point size in 1 pt steps.

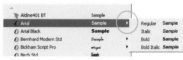

Style

1 To change the style, for example to bold or italic, choose Type>Font. If a choice of style is available, it is indicated by a pop-up triangle to the right of the typeface name in the font list. If there is no pop-up then there are no style options for the typeface.

2 You can also change the style for highlighted text using the Style pop-up menu in the Control palette.

3 To apply settings such as All Caps, Small Caps, Superscript, Subscript, Underline and Strikethrough, click on the appropriate button in the Control palette.

Leading

Leading is a traditional typesetting measurement. It measures the distance from one baseline of type to the next. A baseline is an imaginary line running along the base of type. Leading is an extremely important factor in setting type and can greatly affect the readability of the text on a page.

Leading is set relative to the size of the type with which you are working. For example, if your body text size is 10 points, you might set a leading value of 14 points. This is expressed as ten on fourteen (10/14).

When you enter type into a newly created frame it uses auto-leading as the default leading method. (See below for further information on auto-leading.)

InDesign applies leading as a character attribute. Enter values for leading from 0-5000 points in .001 point accuracy.

Absolute/Fixed Leading

Absolute or Fixed leading uses a fixed value for your leading, which does not vary when you change the point size of your type. For example, if you are working with 9 point type with a leading value of 13 points (9/13), and then change the type size to 12, the leading value remains set at 13.

To set a fixed leading value, first select the text to which you want it to apply – the leading value for a line is set according to the highest leading value applied to any character on the line.

My beautiful fish

My fish shines in the deep blue ocean waves. My fish shines and shimmers when happy. My fish glows and sparkles when it plays games with his friends. My fish bubbles playfully when he talks. My fish loves the coral reef when he swims past.
My fish sparkles like a rainbow in the sky on a rainy day. My fish is very proud of his scales.

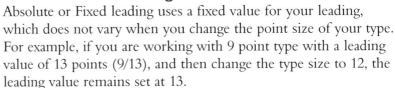

My beautiful fish

My fish shines in the deep blue ocean waves. My fish shines and shimmers when happy. My fish glows and sparkles when it plays games with his friends. My fish bubbles playfully when he talks. My fish loves the coral reef when

You can use the Eyedropper tool to copy type settings. Using the Type tool, highlight the "target" text whose settings you want to change. Select the Eyedropper tool, then click carefully on the "source" text which has the type settings you want to copy. The settings are immediately applied to the target text. Select any other tool in the Toolbox to end the procedure.

2 Make sure the Character Formatting controls button is selected in the Control palette, or use the Character palette (Ctrl/Command+T).

3 Highlight the Leading entry field. Enter a leading value. Press Enter/Return to apply the value to the selected text.

4 You can also use the Leading pop-up to choose from the preset list, or click the arrows (⬍)to increase or decrease the leading in 1-point steps.

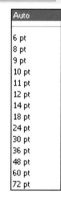

5 To change leading for selected text using the keyboard, hold down the Alt/option key and press the up/down arrow keys on the keyboard. The leading changes in 2-point steps.

Auto-leading

Auto-leading sets a leading value equivalent to an additional 20% of the type size with which you are working. When you decrease or increase the point size of your text, the leading will change automatically to a value that is 20% greater than the new point size. You can choose Auto-leading from the Leading pop-up in the Control palette or the Character palette.

To change the default value for auto-leading, in either the Control palette with the Paragraph Formatting Controls button selected, or the Paragraph palette, choose Justification from the palette menu (▶). Enter a new value for Auto-leading; then click OK.

| To set Auto-leading, make sure you have a range of text selected, and then choose Auto from the Leading pop-up. Auto-leading is represented as a value in brackets.

My beautiful fish

My fish shines in the deep blue ocean waves. My fish shines and shimmers when happy. My fish glows and sparkles when it plays games with his friends. My fish bubbles playfully when he talks. My fish loves the coral reef when he swims past.

My fish sparkles like a rainbow in the sky on a rainy day. My fish is very proud of his scales.

Kerning

Kerning is the technique of reducing the space between certain pairs of characters that do not produce attractive, graceful results when they occur next to one another, especially at larger point sizes. For example, LA, To, P., WA. In InDesign you can use Manual kerning, Optical kerning or Metrics kerning to achieve balanced, attractive spacing.

Manual Kerning

Manual kerning allows you to kern character pairs in 1/1000th Em units, using the Control palette, the Character palette, or keyboard shortcuts.

Choose Edit> Preferences >Units & Increments (Windows), or InDesign>Preferences>Units & Increments (Mac), and enter a value in the Kerning entry field to specify the default Kerning/ Tracking increment when you use the Kerning or Tracking keyboard shortcut:

Keyboard Increments	
Cursor Key:	0.01 39 in
Size/Leading:	1 pt
Baseline Shift:	1 pt
Kerning:	20 /1000 em

1 To manually kern character pairs, first select the Type tool and click to place the Text insertion point between two characters.

2 In the Control palette, enter a value in the Kerning entry field, and press Enter/Return to apply the new value. Alternatively, you can use the Kerning pop-up to choose from the preset list, or you can click the arrows (↕) to adjust the kerning in steps of 10. Negative values move characters closer together; positive values move characters further apart.

Both Kerning and Tracking are measured in units of 1/1000th Em.

3 Hold down Alt/option and press the left or right arrow key to move characters by the default kerning step of 20/1000th of an em. Hold down Ctrl/Command+Alt/option and press the left or right arrow key to kern in steps of 5 times the default amount.

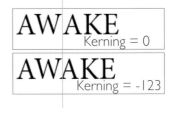

AWAKE Kerning = 0

AWAKE Kerning = -123

You can use the shortcut Ctrl/ Command+Alt/ option+Q to remove all manual tracking and kerning from selected text. Beware: this shortcut also resets the Kerning method to Metrics and removes tracking settings applied through a paragraph style.

4 To remove manual kerning, make sure your text insertion point is flashing between the character pair; then enter a zero in the Kerning entry field.

Metrics Kerning

Use Metrics as the kerning method when you
want to use the pair kerning information built
into a font. Metrics is the default kerning method applied when
you enter text into a new text frame, or when you
first import text.

> To apply Metrics kerning, select the text and choose
> Metrics from the Kerning pop-up in the Control
> or Character palette. A kerning value enclosed in
> brackets, when your text insertion point is flashing
> between character pairs, indicates the kerning
> value used by the Metrics kerning method.

Optical Kerning

The Optical method kerns character pairs visually, and can provide
good results for type consisting of mixed font and size settings.

> Select a range of text to which
> you have applied mixed font
> and size settings. Choose
> Optical from the kerning pop-
> up in the Control palette or
> the Character palette.

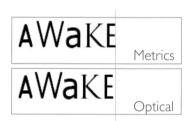

Metrics

Optical

Word Kerning

Word Kerning increases or decreases the space between selected
words. It works by changing the space between the first character
of a word and the space preceding it.

> Use Ctrl/Command+Alt/option+\ (backslash) to increase the
> space between selected words.

> 2 Use Ctrl/Command+Alt/option+Backspace to reduce the space
> between selected words.

Tracking

Tracking, sometimes referred to as "range kerning", is the technique of adding or removing space between characters across a range of text, rather than between individual character pairs. Any tracking amount you specify is in addition to any kerning already in effect.

1. To track a range of text, first select the Type tool, and then highlight the range of text you want to track.

2. Highlight the Tracking entry field in the Control palette or the Character palette, and then enter a value for the amount you want to track. Press Enter/Return to apply the new value. Positive values increase the space between characters; negative values decrease the space.

3. Alternatively, use the Tracking pop-up to choose from the preset list, or click the arrows ( ) to adjust the tracking by the default steps.

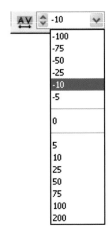

4. If required, choose Edit> Preferences>Composition (Windows), or InDesign>Preferences>Compositi on (Mac), and then select the Custom Tracking/Kerning option to display a highlight color on instances of manual tracking and kerning in your text.

Horizontal and Vertical Scale

InDesign offers controls for both horizontal and vertical scaling of type. Use these controls to expand or condense selected characters. Although not strictly as good as using a true condensed font, these controls can sometimes be useful when working with headlines and when creating special effects with type. The default value for both the Horizontal and Vertical scales is 100%.

Exaggerated Horizontal or Vertical scaling visibly distorts characters, creating pronounced differences between the relative weights of vertical and horizontal strokes in the letterforms:

L

1   To scale type horizontally or vertically, first use the Type tool to select the range of text.

2   Highlight the Vertical or Horizontal entry field in the Control palette or the Character palette, and enter a new value (1.0–1000). Press Enter/Return to apply the change.

3   Alternatively, use the Vertical/Horizontal pop-up menus to choose from the preset list, or click the arrows to adjust the vertical/ horizontal scaling in 1% steps.

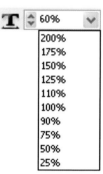

Scaling in action:

PENCIL   Vertical = 100%
Horizontal = 100%

PENCIL   Horizontal = 60%

PENCIL   Vertical = 130%

Baseline Shift and Slanted Text

A baseline is an imaginary line that runs along the base of text characters. It is an important concept when talking about typography. Using the Baseline Shift control you can move highlighted characters above or below their original baseline.

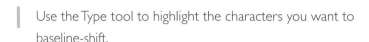

1 Use the Type tool to highlight the characters you want to baseline-shift.

2 Highlight the Baseline Shift entry field in the Control palette or the Character palette, enter a new value, and then press Enter/Return to apply the change. Positive values shift characters upward; negative values shift characters downward. You can also click the arrows ( ) to increase/decrease the baseline shift by the default steps.

Slanted Text

You can use the Skew entry field of the Control palette or the Character palette to slant selected text. This produces an italic-like effect on the text, which is sometimes referred to as "machine italic". To apply a true italic to selected text you must use the Style sub-menu in the Font menu or from the Style pop-up in the Control or Character palette. (See page 63 for further information on selecting type styles.)

Select an individual character or a range of text using the Type tool. Enter a value in the Skew entry field (-85 to 85). Press Enter/Return to apply the new value. A positive value slants the type to the right, and a negative value slants it to the left.

abq 45 degrees

abq -45 degrees

Paragraph Settings

The aim of all good typesetting is to produce attractive, balanced and easily readable type. Understanding and control of the paragraph setting options will help you achieve this goal. The innovative type composition engines available in InDesign make it possible to set attractive, balanced type consistently and easily.

You can use the Control palette or the Paragraph palette to access the complete set of controls for setting paragraph formats.

Covers

Chapter Five

Indents

InDesign allows you to specify left, right and first-line indents. Left and right indents control the start and end position of lines of text relative to the left and right edges of the text frame. This can be useful when you are setting type on a colored background, where you don't want the type to run right up to the edge of the color or tint. First-line indents can be used to indicate visually the start of a new paragraph, and are particularly useful when you are not using additional space between paragraphs.

Use the Control palette or the Paragraph palette to create indents. Make sure you select the Paragraph Formatting Controls button (¶) in the Control palette. If the Paragraph palette is not already showing, choose Type>Paragraph (Ctrl/Command+M).

1 To set a left or right indent, select the Type tool, then select the paragraph(s) to which you want to apply the indents. Highlight the Left/Right indent entry field, enter a new value, and then press Enter/Return to apply the change. You can also click arrows to change the indents in increments.

My beautiful fish
fish shines in the deep blue ocean waves. My fish shines and shimmers when happy. My fish glows and sparkles when it plays games with his friends. My fish bubbles playfully when he talks. My fish loves the coral reef when he swims past. My fish sparkles like a rainbow in the sky on a rainy day. My fish is very proud of his scales.

2 To set a First Line Left Indent, select the paragraph(s) to which you want to apply the indent, and enter a new value in the First Line entry field. Press Enter/Return to apply the change.

My beautiful fish
My fish shines in the deep blue ocean waves. My fish shines and shimmers when happy. My fish glows and sparkles when it plays games with his friends.
My fish bubbles playfully when he talks. My fish loves the coral reef when he swims past.
My fish sparkles like a rainbow in the sky on a rainy day. My fish is very proud of his scales.

To apply the change you have made to an entry field in the Paragraph or Control palette without moving out of the palette, press the Tab key to move the highlight to the next field. Press Shift+Tab to move the highlight back into the previous field if you want to adjust the value again.

3 Even if your unit of measurement is set to inches, you may prefer to set indents in picas and points instead. To set an indent using picas, enter a value followed by a "p"; for example, 1p. To enter a value in points, enter a value followed by "pt"; for example, 6pt. When you press the Enter/Return key to apply the change, the value you have entered is converted to its equivalent in inches.

Space Before/Space After

Space Before/Space After refers to space before or after a paragraph. Use these controls to create additional visual space between paragraphs. For example, Space Before is useful for subheads. Because you create precise amounts of space before or after a paragraph, these controls offer greater flexibility when setting type than entering an additional hard return after a paragraph.

Space Before is not applied if a paragraph begins at the top of a text frame. This prevents unwanted space appearing at the top of the frame. For example, when a subhead with Space Before occurs in this position, you wouldn't normally want the additional space above it.

1 To create space before or after a paragraph, select it using the Type tool. Enter a value in the Space Before/After entry field in the Control palette or the Paragraph palette. Remember to press Enter/Return to apply the change. You can also click the arrows ( ) to change the Space Before/After value in incremental steps.

> ⯅ 0.2 in   ⯅ 0.2 in

ish shines in the deep blue ocean waves. My fish shines and shimmers when happy. My fish glows and sparkles when it plays games with his friends.

My fish bubbles playfully when he talks. My fish loves the coral reef when he swims past.

My fish sparkles like a rainbow in the sky on a rainy day. My fish is very proud of his scales.

2 If you set a fixed leading value for your text (see page 64 for information on leading), you can create the effect of a line space between paragraphs (the equivalent of using a hard return) by setting Space Before or After to the same value as the leading value. To do this, simply enter a value followed by "pt" to specify points, for example 12pt.

> ⯅ 15pt

My fish shines in the deep blue ocean waves. My fish shines and shimmers when happy. My fish glows and sparkles when it plays games with his friends.

My beautiful fish
My fish bubbles playfully when he talks. My fish loves the coral reef when he swims past.
My fish sparkles like a rainbow in the sky on a rainy day. My fish is very proud of his scales.

Alignment

Alignment works at a paragraph level. If your Text insertion point is located in a paragraph, changing the alignment setting changes the alignment for the entire paragraph. Use the Type tool to highlight a range of paragraphs if you want to change the alignment of multiple paragraphs.

1 To change the alignment of some text, select the Type tool; then click into a paragraph to place the Text insertion point, or highlight a range of paragraphs.

2 Click one of the Alignment icons in the Control palette or the Paragraph palette.

My fish shines in the deep blue ocean waves. My fish shines and shimmers when happy. My fish glows and sparkles when it plays games with his firends. My fish bubbles playfully when he talks. My fish loves the coral reef around him.

My fish shines in the deep blue ocean waves. My fish shines and shimmers when happy. My fish glows and sparkles when it plays games with his firends. My fish bubbles playfully when he talks. My fish loves the coral reef around him.

My fish shines in the deep blue ocean waves. My fish shines and shimmers when happy. My fish glows and sparkles when it plays games with his firends. My fish bubbles playfully when he talks. My fish loves the coral reef around him.

Justified Text Options

The variations for justified text are: Justified with last line aligned center; Justify all lines; Justified with last line aligned right.

My fish shines in the deep blue ocean waves. My fish shines and shim-mers when happy. My fish glows and sparkles when it plays games with his firends. My fish bubbles playfully when he talks. My fish loves the coral reef around him.

My fish shines in the deep blue ocean waves. My fish shines and shim-mers when happy. My fish glows and sparkles when it plays games with his firends. My fish bubbles playfully when he talks. My fish loves the coral reef around him.

My fish shines in the deep blue ocean waves. My fish shines and shim-mers when happy. My fish glows and sparkles when it plays games with his firends. My fish bubbles playfully when he talks. My fish loves the coral reef around him.

Align to Spine Options

Use the Align toward/away from Spine buttons in a double-sided document so that text is right-aligned on a left-hand page and left-aligned when it flows onto a right-hand page.

Drop Caps

A drop cap is a paragraph-level attribute. Drop caps can add visual interest to a layout and help to guide the reader to the start of the main text. Drop caps are also often used to break up long passages of running copy in newspaper layouts.

1 To create a drop cap, select the Type tool, then click into a paragraph of text to place the Text insertion point. It is not necessary to highlight the first character in the paragraph.

2 Enter a value in the Drop Cap Number of Lines entry field in the Control palette or the Paragraph palette, to specify the number of lines for the drop cap. Press Enter/Return to apply the change. You can also click the arrows (↕) to change the value in single steps. The bottom of the drop cap aligns with the baseline of the number of lines you enter.

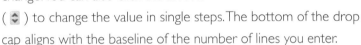

Enter a value in the Drop Cap Number of Characters entry field if you want to "drop" more than one initial character.

Chemical companies are still failing to reali the enormous potential value in the suppl chain. The decision is in line with an anti-dumping investigation started on 6 March last year, it said. It is hard to tell where posturing end and real positions begin. The research also revealed that the chemical supply chain is becoming increasin ly connected and inter-related along its entire length. The headlines of the deal sees pilots taking a 6% pay cut in the year that started on 1 April.
You can visit our websites without telling us who you

3 To make further changes to the appearance of the drop cap, drag across the character to highlight it; then use options in the Control palette or the Character palette to change the settings of the character. You can also apply a different fill color.

See page 121 for information on how you apply a fill color to type.

Chemical com the enormou ply chain. Th antidumping last year, it said. It is ha and real positions begi that the chemical supp ly connected and inter The headlines of the de cut in the year that star

4 To adjust the spacing between the drop cap and the indented lines of type to its right, click to place the Text insertion point between the drop cap and the character that immediately follows it. Use the Kerning field in the Control palette or the Character palette to alter the amount of space. Notice that changing the kerning value affects all the lines of type indented by the drop cap setting.

See page 66 for information on how you can kern character pairs.

Chemical comp the enormous chain. The de dumping inve last year, it said. It is hare and real positions begin. the chemical supply chain nected and inter-related a The headlines of the deal

Aligning to a Baseline Grid

A baseline (or leading) grid is normally set to the leading value of the body text in a publication. Aligning body copy to a predefined baseline grid ensures that baselines of body copy text line up across multiple columns and even spreads – bringing a consistency to typesetting, which is often pleasing and desirable.

Setting a Baseline Grid

Regardless of the Threshold setting in the Grids Preference dialog box, a grid does not show if View>Show Baseline Grid is not selected.

1 To set a baseline grid choose Edit>Preferences>Grids (Windows), or InDesign>Preferences>Grids (Mac). In the Baseline Grid area, use the color pop-up to specify a color for the grid. Specify a threshold value to control the magnification at which the grid becomes visible. For example, if you set a value of 120%, the baseline grid appears at magnifications of only 120% or above.

The keyboard shortcut to show/hide the baseline grid is Ctrl/Command+Alt/option+ ' (apostrophe).

2 Enter a value for the Start position of the grid. For example, this might be zero to start the grid from the top of the page.

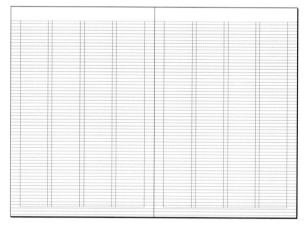

Alternatively, you might enter a value equivalent to the top margin that you set for the document in the New Document dialog box.

...cont'd

In the Increment Every field, enter a number followed by "pt" to specify the baseline grid increment in points.

3 Enter a value in the Increment Every field to specify the distance between the lines in the grid. Normally, the value you enter will be equivalent to the leading value of your body text. This is an important design decision that will affect the entire look of your publication and is usually decided upon before you even begin creating individual pages.

Increment Every: 10pt

Aligning Text to the Grid

1 To align baselines of text to the grid, select the text you want to align.

Although you can lock a paragraph onto the baseline grid by clicking the Align to Grid button with just the Text insertion point flashing in a paragraph, to change the leading of a complete paragraph you must have the whole paragraph selected.

2 Make sure the leading value for the selected text is equal to or less than the Increment Every value set in the Grid preferences dialog box. If the leading value is greater than the value in the Increment Every field the text will lock on to alernating grid increments.

3 Click on the Align to Grid button in the Control palette or the Paragraph palette. The baselines of the selected text align to the grid.

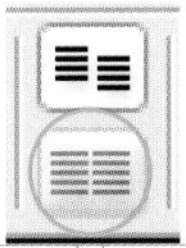

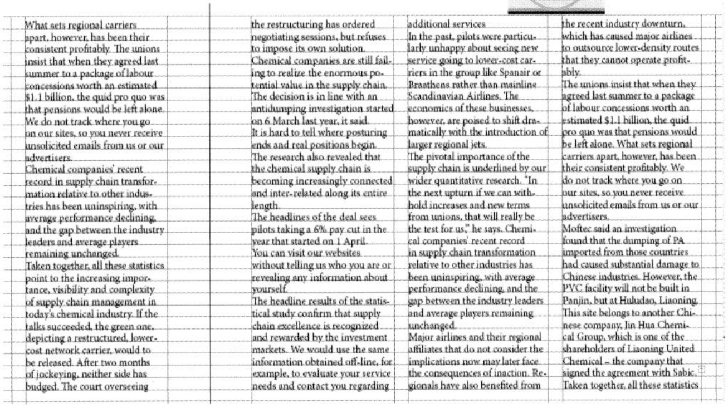

[columns of placeholder text]

Hyphenation

InDesign provides flexible options for controlling hyphenation in both justified and left-aligned text. Hyphenation is a paragraph-level control.

1   To switch hyphenation on or off for a selected paragraph, click the Hyphenate option in the Control palette or the Paragraph palette. Text is hyphenated according to the settings in the Hyphenation dialog box.

☐ Hyphenate

Changing Hyphenation Options

1   Choose Hyphenation from the palette menu (▶) in the Control palette or the Paragraph palette. Clicking the Hyphenate option has the same effect as clicking the Hyphenate option in the Paragraph palette itself – switching hyphenation on or off.

2   Enter a value in the Words with at Least field to specify how long a word must be before InDesign attempts to hyphenate it.

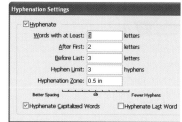

3   Enter a value in the After First entry field to specify the minimum number of letters that must precede a hyphen at the end of a line. For example, a value of 3 will prevent "de-" from occurring at the end of a line. Enter a value in the Before Last field to specify the number of letters that must appear after a hyphen on the new line. For example, a value of 3 will prevent "ed" appearing on a new line.

4   Enter a value in the Hyphen Limit entry field to limit the number of consecutive hyphens. A value of 2 or 3 will prevent the possibility of a "step ladder" effect occurring in justified text in very narrow columns.

It is hard to tell where posturing ends and real positions begin. The research also revealed that the chemical supply chain is becoming increasingly connected and inter-

Click the Preview button to see the results of changes reflected in your text before you OK the dialog box.

5 Use the Hyphenation Zone setting to control hyphenation in left-aligned text using the Single-line composer. The higher the setting, the less hyphenation will be allowed, leading to a more ragged right margin.

6 If necessary, drag the Hyphenation slider to adjust the balance between spacing and hyphenation.

Better Spacing ⬧ Fewer Hyphens

7 Deselect the Hyphenate Capitalized Words option if you want to prevent capitalized words from hyphenating.

If a word contains a discretionary hyphen, InDesign will not hyphenate the word at any other point.

Discretionary Hyphens

1 Select the Type tool. Click to place the Text insertion point where you want to insert the discretionary hyphen. Choose Type>Insert Special Character>Discretionary Hyphen. You can also access the Special Character sub-menu using the context-sensitive menu. Click the right mouse button (Windows), or hold down control and click the mouse button (Mac), to display the context menu. Choose Insert Special Character and then choose Discretionary Hyphen from the sub-menu.

Auto Page Number	Alt+Shift+Ctrl+N
Next Page Number	
Previous Page Number	
Section Marker	
Footnote Number	
Bullet Character	Alt+8
Copyright Symbol	Alt+G
Ellipsis	Alt+;
Paragraph Symbol	Alt+7
Registered Trademark Symbol	Alt+R
Section Symbol	Alt+6
Trademark Symbol	
Em Dash	Alt+Shift+-
En Dash	Alt+-
Discretionary Hyphen	Shift+Ctrl+-
Nonbreaking Hyphen	Alt+Ctrl+-
Double Left Quotation Mark	Alt+[
Double Right Quotation Mark	Alt+Shift+[
Single Left Quotation Mark	Alt+]
Single Right Quotation Mark	Alt+Shift+]
Tab	Tab
Right Indent Tab	Shift+Tab
Indent to Here	Ctrl+\
End Nested Style Here	

Whether a word breaks when you insert a discretionary hyphen depends on the other hyphenation and composition settings in force for the paragraph. You can identify the presence of a discretionary hyphen in a word by showing hidden characters (Type>Show Hidden Characters):

» Cho(o)se·

You can prevent a hyphenated word from hyphenating by entering a discretionary hyphen immediately in front of the word.

2 To insert a discretionary hyphen using the keyboard, hold down Ctrl/Command+Shift, and type a hyphen. If text is edited and reflows so that the hyphenated word moves to another position or into another line, the discretionary hyphen does not appear.

Keep Options

The Keep Options are most useful in longer documents, such as manuals and reports; they control how paragraphs and lines fall at the bottom of columns and pages.

Keep With Next

This control ensures that a subhead does not appear stranded at the bottom of a page or column without any of the subsequent paragraphs to which it relates.

1   To apply Keep with Next, position your Text insertion point in a paragraph such as a subheading. Choose Keep Options from the palette menu (▶) in the Control palette or the Paragraph palette.

2   Enter a value in the Keep with Next entry field. For example, enter a 2 to ensure that if the subhead paragraph is followed by only one line of the next paragraph at the bottom of a column or page, then both the subhead and the single line of text will move to the top of the next column or page.

Keep Lines Together – All Lines in Paragraph

This control prevents paragraphs from splitting across the bottom of a column or page: a few lines of a paragraph appearing at the bottom of a column or page, and the remaining lines continuing at the top of the next column or page.

1   In the Keep Options dialog box, select the Keep Lines Together option. Then select All Lines in Paragraph.

Keep Lines Together – At Start/At End

Use these two controls to prevent Widows and Orphans appearing in your text. InDesign defines an Orphan as the first line of a paragraph that falls at the bottom of a column or page. A Widow is the last line of a paragraph falling at the top of a column or page. Enter a value that defines the number of lines that is acceptable at the bottom or top of a column or page.

1   To prevent an Orphan from appearing at the bottom of a column or page, enter a value of 2 or more in the Start entry field. (Start refers to the starting lines of a paragraph.) For example, a value of 3 means that either one or two lines at the start of a paragraph that occur at the bottom of a column or a page would constitute an orphan, and they are therefore automatically moved to the top of the next page or column.

2   To prevent a Widow from appearing at the top of a column or page, enter a value of 2 or greater in the End entry field. For example, a value of 2 means that a single line at the top of a column or page constitutes a Widow. Lines of text are moved from the bottom of the preceding column or page to the top of the next column or page.

Column and Page Breaks

In longer documents, such as reports and manuals, it is often useful to specify column and page breaks automatically.

1 To ensure that a paragraph starts at the top of a column, select the Type tool; then click into the paragraph to place the Text insertion point. Choose Keep Options (Ctrl/Command+Alt/option+K) from the Control palette or Paragraph palette menu. Choose In Next Column or In Next Frame from the Start Paragraph pop-up. If you are working with a series of threaded text frames, choosing In Next Column or In Next frame produces the same result.

The unions insist that when they agreed last summer to a package of labour concessions worth an estimated $1.1 billion, the quid pro quo was that pensions would be left alone. We do not track where you go on our sites, so you never receive unsolicited emails from us or our advertisers.
Chemical companies' recent record in supply chain transformation relative to other industries has been uninspiring, with average performance declining, and the gap between the industry leaders and average players remaining unchanged.

Chemical Statistics Revealed
Taken together, all these statistics point to the increasing importance, visibility and complexity of supply chain management in today's chemical industry. If the talks succeeded, the green one, depicting a restructured, lower-cost network carrier, would to be released. After two months of jockeying, neither side has budged. The court overseeing the restructuring has ordered negotiating sessions, but refuses to impose its own solution.
Chemical companies are still failing to realize the enormous potential value in the supply chain. The decision is in line with an antidumping investigation started on 6 March last year, it said.

It is hard to tell where posturing ends and real positions begin. The research also revealed that the chemical supply chain is becoming increasingly connected and inter-related along its entire length.
The headlines of the deal sees pilots taking a 6% pay cut in the year that started on 1 April.
You can visit our websites without telling us who you are or revealing any information about yourself.
The headline results of the statistical study confirm that supply chain excellence is recognized and rewarded by the investment markets. We would use the same information obtained off-line, for example, to evaluate your service needs and contact you regarding

2 To ensure that a paragraph starts at the top of the next page, select the Type tool; then click into the paragraph to place the Text insertion point. Choose Keep Options from the Control palette or Paragraph palette menu. Choose On Next Page from the Start Paragraph pop-up menu.

3 Use On Next Odd Page/On Next Even Page in long documents when you want a particular heading style, such as a chapter heading, to always begin on a left- or right-hand page.

Text Composers

The aim of good typesetting is to create an even, balanced tone or color on your page – achieved by the consistent, balanced spacing of type in columns. Most desktop publishing systems allow you to specify a range of typographic controls and settings that attempt to create this result by considering word spacing, letter spacing and hyphenation options one line at a time.

Adobe InDesign can offer enhanced results through the use of a multi-line text composer, which uses algorithms to rank possible line breaks, spacing and hyphenation options, not only for a single line, but for an entire paragraph. Unlike traditional typesetting systems, it has the ability to scan forward and backward. The result is evenly spaced lines with optimal line breaks. The Adobe Paragraph composer is selected by default.

Switching Composers

If you need to you can choose to use the Single-line composer.

The palette menu button for palettes docked in the palette bar appears in the top-left corner of the palette. The palette menu button for the Control palette is located to the far right of the palette. In floating palettes, the palette menu button is located in the top-right corner. The appearance of the button is identical in all instances:

To choose the Single-line composer, highlight the range of text you want to work on, and choose Single-line Composer from the Paragraph palette menu. Alternatively, with the Paragraph Formatting Controls button (¶) selected, choose Justification from the Control palette menu. Select Single-line Composer from the Composer pop-up menu.

Paragraph Composer	Single-line Composer
The unions insist that when they agreed last summer to a package of concessions worth an estimated $1.1 billion, the quid pro quo was that pensions would be left alone. We do not track where you go on our sites, so you never receive unsolicited emails from us or our advertisers. Chemical companies' recent record in supply chain transformation relative to other industries has been uninspiring, with average performance declining, and the gap between the industry leaders and average players remaining unchanged.	The unions insist that when they agreed last summer to a package of concessions worth an estimated $1.1 billion, the quid pro quo was that pensions would be left alone. We do not track where you go on our sites, so you never receive unsolicited emails from us or our advertisers. Chemical companies' recent record in supply chain transformation relative to other industries has been uninspiring, with average performance declining, and the gap between the industry leaders and average players remaining unchanged.

Setting Composer Preferences

You can use the Composition preferences to control whether or not problem lines are indicated visually on screen.

1   To set highlight options to indicate where InDesign is unable to honor word spacing, letter spacing and Keep options, as well as instances of manual kerning and tracking, choose Edit> Preferences>Composition (Windows), or InDesign>Preferences> Composition (Mac).

2   Select Keep Violations if you want InDesign to highlight any instances where Keep Option settings cannot be honored.

Composition

Highlight
- ☐ Keep Violations   ☑ Substituted Fonts
- ☐ H&J Violations   ☐ Substituted Glyphs
- ☐ Custom Tracking/Kerning

Text Wrap
- ☐ Justify Text Next to an Object
- ☑ Skip By Leading
- ☐ Text Wrap Only Affects Text Ber

3   Select H&J Violations if you want InDesign to highlight instances where Hyphenation and Justification settings cannot be honored. InDesign uses three shades of yellow to highlight problems. The more serious the violation, the darker yellow the highlight color.

The headlines of the deal sees pilots taking a 6% pay cut in the year that started on 1 April.
You can visit our websites without telling us who you are or revealing any information about yourself.
The headline results of the statistical study confirm that supply chain excellence is recognized and rewarded by the investment markets. We would use the same information obtained off-line, for example, to evaluate your service needs and contact you regarding additional services.

4   Select Custom Tracking/Kerning to highlight instances of manual kerning or tracking in green.

5   Select the Substituted Fonts option if you want InDesign to highlight any substitute fonts in pink. This option is on by default.

Paragraph Rules

Paragraph rules are a paragraph attribute. Use paragraph rules above, below, or above and below a paragraph, when you want the rule to flow with copy as it is edited and reflows.

You can set up paragraph rules on individual paragraphs, or you can set them up as part of a paragraph style.

1 Using the Type tool, highlight the paragraph(s) to which you want to apply the paragraph rule. Choose Paragraph Rules (Ctrl/Command+Alt/option+J) from the palette menu in either the Paragraph or Control palette.

2 Choose to set either a Rule Above or Rule Below from the pop-up. Select the Rule On checkbox. Select the Preview checkbox to see settings applied as you create them.

You can enter values to .01 point accuracy in the Weight entry field.

The Color list contains all the colors currently available in the Swatches palette, so it is a good idea to define a color for rules beforehand if necessary.

3 Enter a Weight, or use the Weight pop-up to choose from the preset list. Choose a color for the rule from the Color pop-up.

4 Use the Width pop-up to specify the (horizontal) length of the rule. The Column option creates a rule that is the width of the column, regardless of any left or right indents that might be set for the paragraphs. The Text option creates a variable-width rule that is the length of the text in the paragraph. If you apply a Text paragraph rule below a paragraph consisting of more than one line, the rule is the length of the last line of text in the paragraph.

new concept shop.

New Sites Set

The new company is looking
for a site in new concept shop.
also consid
mainland **New Sites Set**

The new company is looking
for a site in London, but would
also consider opening in
mainland Europe if a suitable

5　You can specify left and right indents for rules that are the width of the column or the width of the text. A left indent moves the start of the rule in from the left; a right indent moves the end of the rule in from the right.

6　Specify an Offset value to position the top of a Rule Below, or the bottom of a Rule Above, relative to the baseline of the paragraph. For example, a value of zero for a Rule Below positions the top of the rule on the baseline of the paragraph. A value of zero for a Rule Above positions the bottom of the rule on the baseline.

A "baseline" is an imaginary line that runs along the base of characters in a line of type.

Reverse Paragraph Rules

A popular and useful effect that you can create using paragraph rules is to reverse text out of a paragraph rule. Typically, reversed-out rules are used on subheads and in tables where alternate colors are used to distinguish rows from one another.

1　Choose Paragraph Rules from the palette menu in the Paragraph or Control palette. You can use either a Rule Above or Below to achieve the effect. Select the Rule On checkbox to switch the effect on. Specify a line weight that is slightly greater than the point size of the type in the paragraph and choose a color that contrasts with the color of the type.

When you create a reverse rule on a paragraph sitting at the top of a text frame, the reverse rule may extend upward, beyond the top of the frame. You may have to reposition the text frame slightly to get the top of the rule to line up exactly where you want it.

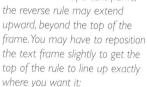

2　Set width and indents as desired. Specify a negative offset for the rule to position the text visually in the middle of the rule. You will need to experiment with the exact offset to get it right.

Images and Graphic Frames

Images add impact to the majority of publications. Adobe InDesign treats scanned pictures and bitmap images from applications such as Adobe Photoshop and Paint Shop Pro in the same way as vector artwork that you might create in an application such as Adobe Illustrator or CorelDRAW™.

InDesign can import the following file formats: TIFF, EPS, DCS, JPEG, PDF, GIF, PNG, BMP, PICT, WMF, EMF and CT, as well as Adobe Illustrator and Adobe Photoshop files in their native file formats.

Covers

Chapter Six

Placing an Image

For information on drawing, resizing and moving frames see Chapter 2.

The Place command is the recommended method for importing bitmap or vector graphics, as it provides the greatest support for file formats, image resolution and color data stored in the graphic file.

If you do not select Show Import Options, InDesign uses the default settings, or the last settings used for a graphic file of the type you are importing.

Click on an image with the Selection tool to display useful information such as color space, resolution and file type in the Info palette (F8):

Once you have created your vector artwork in a drawing application, or scanned an image and saved it on your hard disk, you can then import it into a graphic frame.

1   To place an image, select a graphic frame using the Selection tool, and choose File>Place. Use standard Windows/Mac techniques to navigate to the image file you want to place.

2   Click on the image file name to select it. Select Show Import Options if you want to display an additional options dialog box for the image after you click the Open button. Click Open, or double-click the file name; the image appears in the selected frame.

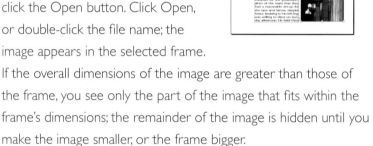

If the overall dimensions of the image are greater than those of the frame, you see only the part of the image that fits within the frame's dimensions; the remainder of the image is hidden until you make the image smaller, or the frame bigger.

3   An alternative to placing an image into a selected frame is to choose File>Place with nothing selected. Select the image file you want to place; then click Open. Position the Loaded graphic cursor where you want the top left edge of the image; then click. The image is automatically placed in a picture frame that fits the size of the image exactly. Using this technique you see the full extent of the image from the outset.

Fitting Options

When you first create a graphic frame and import an image into it, the size of the frame and the size of the image are likely to be different. You can scale the image and the frame using a variety of techniques to suit your purpose. The following steps use options in the Fitting sub-menu.

Fit Content to Frame	Alt+Ctrl+E
Fit Frame to Content	Alt+Ctrl+C
Centre Content	Shift+Ctrl+E
Fit Content Proportionally	Alt+Shift+Ctrl+E
Fill Frame Proportionally	Alt+Shift+Ctrl+C

To control the display quality of images, choose an option from the View>Display Performance sub-menu. The default setting is typical. Choose High Quality to improve the display of high-resolution images and vector artwork on screen:

If your document contains a lot of transparency effects or high-resolution images, High Quality can slow down screen redraw times.

To center an image in a frame choose Object> Fitting>Center Content (Ctrl/ Command+Shift+E):

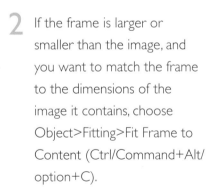

1. If the image is larger or smaller than the frame you place it in, you can choose Object>Fitting>Fit Content Proportionally (Ctrl/ Command+Alt/option+Shift+E). This will scale either the width or the height of the image to fit the dimensions of the frame. This option fits only one dimension, in order to keep the image in proportion.

2. If the frame is larger or smaller than the image, and you want to match the frame to the dimensions of the image it contains, choose Object>Fitting>Fit Frame to Content (Ctrl/Command+Alt/ option+C).

3. To enlarge or shrink the image to exactly the same size as the frame you can choose Object>Fitting>Fit Content to Frame (Ctrl/ Command+Alt/option+E). Beware: this is likely to scale the image non-proportionally.

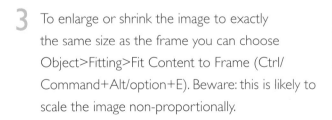

Scaling and Cropping Images

The image in a frame and the frame itself can be manipulated independently. This can be useful when you need to enlarge the image whilst maintaining the size and position of the frame. You can also reposition the image relative to the frame, to control which part of the image appears on your page and prints.

Using the Selection tool

The key to working with images is understanding the way you select and work on the frame, or select and work on the image.

1 To select and work on the frame, use the Selection tool and click on the frame. The selection bounding box appears, indicating the dimensions of the frame; it has eight selection handles around its perimeter.

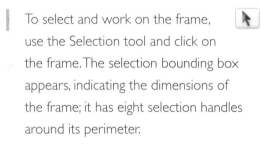

2 Press and drag on a selection handle to change the dimensions of the frame; this does not affect the size of the image.

3 To scale the frame and the image simultaneously, while maintaining the proportions of both: using the Selection tool, hold down Ctrl/Command+Shift and drag a handle.

4 You can also use the W (Width) and H (Height) entry fields in the Control palette to change the dimensions of the frame and the image inside it. Make sure the Constrain Proportions button is selected, enter a value in the W/H entry fields; then press Enter/Return to apply the change.

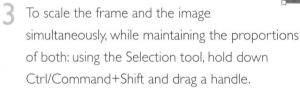

5 To scale the frame and the image inside as a percentage, enter a value in the Scale X/Y Percentage fields. Press Enter/Return to

apply the change. To scale the frame and the image inside it in proportion, first select the Constrain Proportions button in the Control palette; then enter a value in either the Scale X or Scale Y entry field and press Enter/Return. After you press Enter/Return, the values in the Scale X/Y Percentage fields return to 100%.

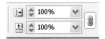

Using the Direct Selection tool

The Direct Selection tool allows you to control and manipulate the image within the frame independently of the frame itself. You can change the size of the image without changing the size of the frame and you can reposition the image within the frame.

1 To select and work on an image independently of its frame, select the Direct Selection tool. Click somewhere inside the image. A boundary box representing the dimensions of the image appears, with eight resize handles around the perimeter. Drag a handle to resize the image. Hold down Shift and drag a handle to resize the image and maintain its original proportions.

2 You can also use the Scale X Percentage / Scale Y Percentage entry fields in the Control or Transform palette. Enter a new value and press Enter/Return to apply the change. When working with the Direct Selection tool, the Scale X/Y Percentage fields represent scaling as a percentage of the original size of the image.

3 To reposition an image within its frame, with the Direct Selection tool selected, position your cursor within the image; then press and drag. The image, not the frame, moves.

Stroking a Frame

The blue selection bounding box into which you place images is a non-printing guide. Regard the frame as an invisible container for the image. There will be times when you will want to apply either a keyline – a thin black outline on the picture – or a thicker, more obvious frame that will print.

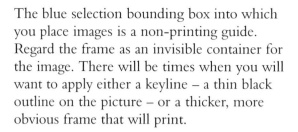

1 To specify a printing frame for a graphic or text frame, first select the frame using the Selection tool.

2 Click the Stroke box in the Toolbox to indicate that you want to apply a stroke color. Click on a color in the Swatches palette to change the color of the frame or stroke.

You can apply a stroke that is centered on the path, which is the same as the method used in Adobe Illustrator:

Or you can apply a stroke on the inside of the path, which is the method that most QuarkXPress users are familiar with. Using this method means that the overall dimensions of the frame do not increase when you apply the stroke:

3 Use the Stroke palette to specify a thickness for the stroke in points. Either enter a value in the Weight entry field and press Enter/Return to apply the change, or use the pop-up to choose from the preset list.

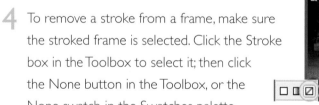

4 To remove a stroke from a frame, make sure the stroked frame is selected. Click the Stroke box in the Toolbox to select it; then click the None button in the Toolbox, or the None swatch in the Swatches palette.

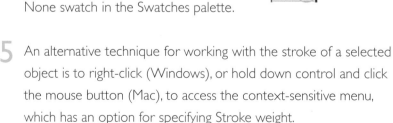

5 An alternative technique for working with the stroke of a selected object is to right-click (Windows), or hold down control and click the mouse button (Mac), to access the context-sensitive menu, which has an option for specifying Stroke weight.

Image Links

A "link" is created automatically when you import an image.

When you import an image using the Place command, InDesign does not automatically embed all the image file information within the document; instead, it creates a link to the original file. On screen you see a low resolution screen preview of the original file. It is very important for printing purposes that links to imported images remain accurate and unbroken: when you print your document, InDesign references the complete, original image file information, to print it accurately and at its correct resolution. Maintaining unbroken links is vital when working with high-resolution images.

Generally speaking, a high-resolution image is one that has been scanned or created at 300ppi (pixels per inch) or greater.

1 To view and manage links after you import images, choose Window>Links (Ctrl/Command+Shift+D). Placed images are listed in the palette, together with their page numbers.

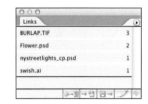

In some cases, you may work with low-resolution images (72–100ppi), which are used to indicate position and size in your layout. Your commercial printer will then need to create the necessary high-resolution images and substitute these for the low-resolution images before outputting the file.

2 Click on an image in the document. The matching entry is highlighted in the Links palette. Choose Link Information from the Links palette menu () to get details on the image, such as Name, Status, Size and Color Space. Click the Previous/Next buttons to cycle through the images in the Links palette. You can use the Relink button to relink to a missing image.

3 Click on a linked file in the Links palette; then choose Embed from the palette menu to store the entire file within the InDesign document. This will add to the file size of the document. Embedded images display an "embedded" icon in the Links palette.

Managing Links

An up-to-date, unmodified image appears in the Links palette indicated by its file name and the page on which it is placed. The links palette also indicates any problems with links.

Relinking

When you relink a placed image, any transformations (for example, rotation), applied to the image within InDesign are maintained and applied to the relinked image.

If an image file has been moved to a different location on your hard disk or network since it was placed, the link is effectively broken – InDesign does not know where it has been moved to. A broken link is indicated by a red circle with a question mark.

To relink to the image so that InDesign is able to access the complete file information for printing, click on the missing file in the Links palette. Either click the Relink button, or choose Relink from the Links palette menu (▶).

2 Use standard Windows/Macintosh navigation windows to locate the missing file. Select the file; then click Open (Windows), or Choose (Mac), to re-establish the link.

You can control the order in which link entries appear in the Links palette by choosing a Sort option from the Links palette menu:

Sort by Name
Sort by Page
✔ Sort by Status

3 You can also use the Relink button or command to replace one image with another. Follow the procedure for relinking, but choose a different file to link to.

Updating

If you have worked on an image since it was originally placed in the document, InDesign recognizes that the file has been modified. For example, you may have placed an image and at a later stage reworked part of it in the application where the image was initially created. A modified image is indicated by a yellow triangle with an exclamation mark.

To update a modified image, click on the modified link in the Links palette to select it. Click the Update

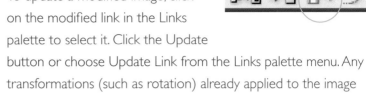

button or choose Update Link from the Links palette menu. Any transformations (such as rotation) already applied to the image are applied to the updated image.

Editing Linked Images

While you are working on a document, you may need to make changes to a placed image. To use the following technique, you must have enough RAM available on your system.

If a file has been moved and updated, you will have to first relink the file and then update it.

To update a placed image, click on the image name in the Links palette; then either click the Edit Original

button, or choose Edit Original from the palette menu. This will launch the application in which the image was originally created, provided that it is installed on your computer system.

Viewing Linked Images

You sometimes need to view an image before you make decisions about relinking, updating or editing.

To view a linked image, click on the image name in the links palette. Click the Go to Link button, or

choose Go to Link from the palette menu. InDesign moves to the appropriate page, selects the image, and centers it in the active window.

2 Alternatively, hold down Alt/option and double-click a file name in the links palette to go to the linked image.

Clipping Paths

A clipping path is a vector path that is used in association with an image to define areas of the image that will appear on the page and print. You can create clipping paths in Adobe Photoshop and other image-editing applications, and you can also generate clipping paths from within InDesign.

You can import a clipping path for files saved in Photoshop, TIFF and EPS file formats.

1   To import an image with a clipping path created in Adobe Photoshop, choose File>Place. Use standard Windows/Mac techniques to navigate to the file you want to place. Click on the file name to select it; then select the Show Import Options option. Click the Open button.

Areas of the image inside the clipping path appear and print; areas outside the clipping path are invisible and do not print.

2   In the secondary Image Import Options dialog box, select the Apply Photoshop Clipping Path option. (If the option is dimmed, the image does not have a clipping path.) Click the OK button.

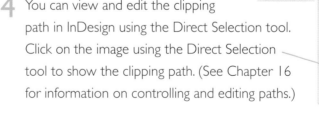

3   The image appears, its visibility defined by the clipping path.

4   You can view and edit the clipping path in InDesign using the Direct Selection tool. Click on the image using the Direct Selection tool to show the clipping path. (See Chapter 16 for information on controlling and editing paths.)

To change a clipping path into a graphic frame, right-click (Windows), or Control+click (Mac), on the image. Choose Convert Clipping Path to Frame from the context menu:

5   If you make changes to an imported clipping path, you can revert back to the original imported path by choosing Object>Clipping Path (Ctrl/Command+Alt/option+Shift+K). Choose Photoshop Path from the Type pop-up.

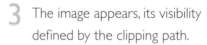

Generating InDesign Clipping Paths

You can also create clipping paths on images from within InDesign. This technique works best on images that have solid white or black backgrounds.

To see the most accurate representation of an image possible, choose View>Display Performance> High Quality Display (Ctrl/ Command+Alt/option+H).

1 To create an InDesign clipping path, select an image with a more or less solid white or black background.

2 Choose Object>Clipping Path. Start by using the default settings; then adjust and fine-tune settings to get the result you require.

3 Drag the threshold slider, or enter a Threshold value, to specify how close to white the pixels must be for them to be hidden outside the clipping path. Low settings ignore white or very near white pixels; higher settings remove a wider range of pixels.

4 Use the Tolerance setting in conjunction with the Threshold setting. Drag the Tolerance slider, or enter a Tolerance value, to specify how tightly the path is drawn. Generally speaking, lower Tolerance values create a rougher, more detailed clipping path with more points. Higher Tolerance values create a smoother, less accurate path with fewer points. You need to experiment with this setting on an image-by-image basis to get the best results.

The default measurement system for the Inset Frame control is millimeters. You can enter a value followed by "pt" if you want to override the default measurement system and work with points instead.

The Invert option can produce interesting special effects. Invert switches the visible and invisible areas defined by the clipping path. In this example, the original white background remains opaque, whereas the area of the lamp becomes see-through:

5 Enter a value in the Inset Frame field to move the path inward. Shrinking a path inward can sometimes help to avoid a slight color fringe around the edge of the clipped image. This is a uniform adjustment for the entire clipping path. You can enter a negative value to expand the path.

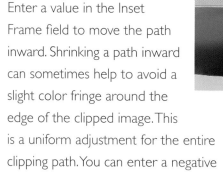
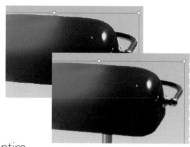

6 Select Include Inside Edges to allow InDesign to create a clipping path that includes areas inside the initial clipping path if there are pixels that fall inside the Tolerance setting. In this example, it was then necessary to reduce the Threshold value so that the highlight area on the lampshade was not included in the clipping path.

7 Select the Restrict to Frame option to prevent the clipping path extending beyond the boundaries of the graphic frame that contains the image. This can create a less complex clipping path in some instances.

8 Switch off the Use High Resolution Image option if you want to create a clipping path quickly, but less precisely, using the screen preview resolution. Leave the option selected for InDesign to use the pixel information in the actual image file to calculate the clipping path with maximum precision.

Image Visibility Controls

Use the Object Layer Options dialog box to control layer and layer comp visibility for layered Photoshop or PDF files placed in InDesign. In Photoshop, a layer comp is a version of an image that records the visibility and position of layers for a particular state of the image. Using layer comps in Photoshop means that you can retain permutations of an image in a single image file. The Object Layer Options dialog box in InDesign allows you to control which layer comp appears in the InDesign document.

1 For a selected Photoshop image that contains layer information, choose Object>Object Layer Options.

2 In the Show Layers scroll box, click on the eye icon to hide the contents of the layer in InDesign. Click the empty eye icon box, (the eye icon appears) to make the contents of the layer visible.

3 In the Update Link Options area, use the When Updating Link pop-up menu to determine how any changes to layer visibility made

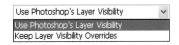

in the original Photoshop file affect the image placed in InDesign when you update the link. (See pages 94–95 for information on updating image links). Select Use Photoshop's Layer Visibility to apply changes made in the Photoshop file, or choose Keep Layer Visibility Overrides to retain any of the layer visibility settings already created for the image in InDesign.

4 Click OK when you are satisfied with your settings.

5 For a selected Photoshop image which contains Layer Comp information, use the Layer Comp pop-up menu to select different Layer Comp states. The visibility icons in the Show Layers area change according to the layer comp you choose.

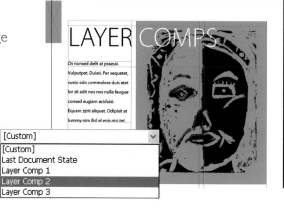

A layer visibility eye icon appears in the Links palette to indicate images with layer visibility overrides:

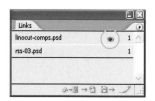

Arranging Objects

As you add more and more objects to a document, the exact arrangement, positioning and alignment of these objects becomes more and more critical. This chapter covers techniques such as aligning and spacing objects, and controlling whether objects appear in front of or behind other objects. It also covers the Layers palette and working with groups of objects.

Covers

Chapter Seven

Stacking Order

When you work with layers (see pages 103–110), stacking order works on a layer-by-layer basis. When you bring an object to the front or send it to the back you are bringing it to the front or sending it to the back for that layer only.

Stacking order refers to the positioning of objects on the page, either in front of or behind other objects. Stacking order becomes apparent when objects overlap. Controlling stacking order is an essential aspect of creating page layouts.

The order in which you create, paste or place objects determines their initial stacking order. The first object you create or place is backmost in the stacking order; each additional object added to the page is stacked in front of all the existing objects.

You can use keyboard shortcuts to control stacking order for selected objects. The shortcuts are listed in the Arrange sub-menu, next to each individual command.

1 To bring an object to the front, first select the object using the Selection tool. Choose Object>Arrange>Bring to Front. To move an object to the back, choose Object>Arrange>Send to Back.

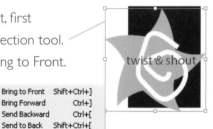

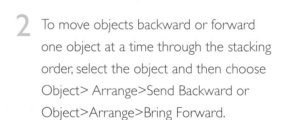

You can access the Arrange sub-menu using the Context menu. Select an object using the Selection tool; then right-click on the object (Windows), or hold down the control key and then click on the object (Mac), to display a context-sensitive menu.

2 To move objects backward or forward one object at a time through the stacking order, select the object and then choose Object> Arrange>Send Backward or Object>Arrange>Bring Forward.

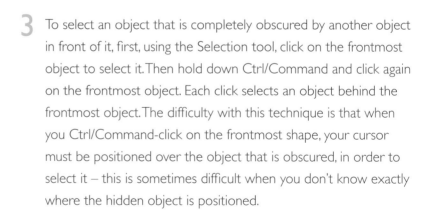

3 To select an object that is completely obscured by another object in front of it, first, using the Selection tool, click on the frontmost object to select it. Then hold down Ctrl/Command and click again on the frontmost object. Each click selects an object behind the frontmost object. The difficulty with this technique is that when you Ctrl/Command-click on the frontmost shape, your cursor must be positioned over the object that is obscured, in order to select it – this is sometimes difficult when you don't know exactly where the hidden object is positioned.

You can also select objects above and below the selected object by using the Select sub-menu. Select an object, and then choose Object>Select. Choose from the options indicated in the screenshot:

First Object Above	⌥⇧⌘]
Next Object Above	⌥⌘]
Next Object Below	⌥⌘[
Last Object Below	⌥⇧⌘[

Creating Layers

Using layers can give you flexibility and control when building complex documents. For example, if you are creating a document with several language versions but a standard layout, you might assign the text for each language to a different layer. You can hide and show individual layers, lock layers against accidental change, control printing for layers and move objects between layers.

When you begin work in a new document you are working on Layer 1 by default. Simple, straightforward documents such as leaflets and flyers probably do not need additional layers.

The keyboard shortcut for showing/hiding the Layers palette is F7.

1 To create a new layer, make sure the Layers palette is visible: choose Window>Layers, or click the Layers tab in the Palette bar. Then choose New Layer from the Layers palette menu ( ). In the New Layer dialog box enter a name for the layer.

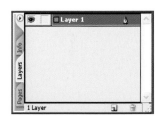

Double-click on a layer name in the Layers palette to show the Layer Options dialog box. The options available are the same as those in the New Layer dialog box.

2 If you want to, choose a different highlight color for the layer from the Color pop-up. When you select an object on the layer, the highlight bounding box appears in this color. This is helpful for identifying the exact layer on which an object is located.

3 Choose suitable Show, Lock and Guides options for the layer. These settings are not permanent and can be changed at any time, either by returning to the New Layer dialog box (by clicking on the layer name and choosing Layer Options from the Layers palette menu) or by using icons in the Layers palette.

The "active" layer is highlighted in the layers palette. A "Pen" icon also indicates the active layer. There can be only one active layer at a time. When you create, paste or place an object in a document with multiple layers, it appears on the active layer.

4 When you create a new layer, it appears above all other existing layers in the Layers palette. Hold down Ctrl/Command and click the New Layer button ( ) to create a new layer above the currently active layer.

Options

Show Layer – select Show Layer to make the layer visible as soon as you create it. Visible layers print by default. You can also click the Eye icon in the left column of the Layers palette to hide or show a layer.

Lock Layer – select Lock Layer to lock the layer as soon as you create it. A locked layer has a pencil with a line through it in the Lock/Unlock column. You can also click in the Lock/Unlock column in the palette to control the Lock status of a layer.

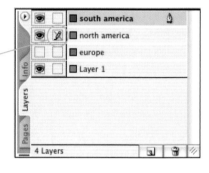

Show Guides – select Show Guides to make the ruler guides you create on the layer visible. When you hide or show a layer, you also hide or show the layer's ruler guides.

Lock Guides – select Lock Guides to immediately lock any guides you create on the new layer. This prevents changes to all ruler guides on the layer.

Suppress Text Wrap When Layer is Hidden – this allows you to control whether or not text wrap settings for objects on the layer remain in force, or are suppressed, when the layer is hidden.

5 Alternatively, click the Create New Layer button at the bottom of the Layers palette. This creates a new layer with a default layer name and uses the last settings used in the New Layer dialog box.

Understanding Layers

If a layer is locked you cannot click on an object on that layer to make the layer active. Unlock the layer first.

In a document with multiple layers you can have only one "active" layer. The active layer is highlighted in the layers palette and has a Pen icon to the right of the layer name. When you draw, paste or place a new object, it is automatically placed on the active layer.

1 To make a layer active, make sure the Layers palette is showing (Window>Layers, or click the Layers tab in the Palette bar); then click on the layer name in the Layers palette. The layer is

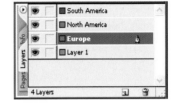

highlighted and a Pen icon appears to the right of the layer name.

Only one layer can be active at a time.

2 You can also click on an object in the document to select the layer on which the object is located. When you select an object on a layer, a small colored dot appears to the right of the layer name. You can use this dot to move objects between layers (see page 106).

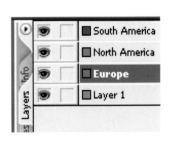

To select all objects on a layer, hold down Alt/ option, and click the layer name.

3 The colored square to the left of the layer name indicates the color of the highlight bounding box for a selected object on that layer. (This color is set when you create the layer – see page 103.)

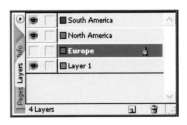

You cannot create, paste or place a new object on a hidden or locked layer. A warning prompt appears if you attempt any of these actions:

4 If you make the active layer invisible, by clicking on the Eye icon, a red line appears through its Pen icon and you cannot draw, paste, or place objects on the layer. Make the layer visible to continue working on it.

Moving Objects from Layer to Layer

InDesign provides a number of techniques for moving objects between layers.

1 To move an object to a different layer, select the object using the Selection tool. The layer on which the object is located becomes highlighted in the Layers palette and a small, colored dot appears to the right of the Pen icon.

2 Drag the dot to a different layer to move the object to that layer. When you release the mouse, the layer you release on becomes the active layer and the object moves to it. The selection handles and the bounding box around the selected object change to the highlight color for that layer. When you move an object to a different layer, it becomes the frontmost object on that layer. You can use the same technique for multiple selected objects or groups on the same layer.

3 You can also cut or copy objects to the clipboard, before pasting them to a different layer. First, make sure that Paste Remembers Layers is not selected in the Layers palette menu ( ). Select the objects you want to move; then choose Edit>Cut/Copy. In the Layers palette, select the layer onto which you want to move the object. Choose Edit>Paste to paste the object onto the layer. It will appear in the center of your screen area. Choose Edit>Paste in Place to paste the object onto the layer at exactly the same position as that from which it was cut or copied.

Managing Layers

There is a range of useful techniques you need to be aware of to work efficiently with layers, including hiding/showing, locking/unlocking, copying, deleting, and changing the order of layers. You can also merge layers together, consolidating separate layers into a single layer.

When you release the mouse, the moved layer becomes the active layer.

To change the layer order, position your cursor on the layer you want to move; then press and drag upward or downward. A thick, black bar indicates where the layer will be positioned when you release the mouse button. Moving a layer upward positions objects on that layer in front of objects on layers that come below it in the Layers palette. Moving a layer downward moves objects on that layer behind objects on layers that appear above it in the Layers palette.

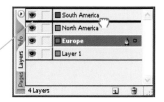

Copying Layers

To copy a layer and its contents, make sure you select the layer you want to copy, and then choose Duplicate Layer from the palette menu.

2 You can also make a copy of a layer and its contents by dragging an existing layer down onto the New Layer button at the bottom of the Layers palette.

Merging Layers

Merge layers when you want to consolidate objects appearing on different layers into the same layer.

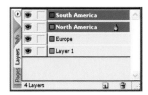

Select two or more layers that you want to combine into a single layer.

2 To select a consecutive range of layers, click on the first layer name you want to select, hold down Shift, and then click on the last layer name. All layers from the first layer you select to the layer on which you Shift+click are selected.

3 To select non-consecutive layers, select a layer, and then hold down Ctrl/Command and click on other layer names to add them to the selection.

4 Choose Merge Layers from the Layers palette menu (▶). When you merge layers, the combined layer retains the name and position of the topmost of the merged layers.

Merge Layers
Delete Unused Layers

Deleting Layers

You can delete empty layers, or layers containing objects, when they are no longer needed.

1 To delete a layer, click on the layer you want to delete. Choose Delete Layer from the Layer palette menu, or click the Wastebasket icon at the bottom of the palette. You can also drag the layer name onto the Wastebasket icon. If there are objects on the layer, a warning dialog box appears indicating that these objects will be deleted. OK the dialog box to delete the layer. If the layer does not contain any objects, the layer is deleted immediately without a warning.

Adobe InDesign

⚠ The layer "europe copy" contains one or more objects. Delete the layer anyway?

OK   Cancel

2 Choose Delete Unused Layers from the Layers palette menu to delete all layers in the document that do not contain any objects.

Hiding and Locking Layers

You can specify whether layers are hidden or visible, locked or unlocked when you first create them; you can then hide/show, and lock/unlock layers as necessary as you build your document.

Hiding Layers

Hidden layers do not print.

Hiding layers is a useful technique when objects overlap and obscure other objects below them in the layering order. You can also hide layers to control the printing of elements in a document. If you are creating a multi-language publication with a consistent layout, but text in different languages held on separate layers, hiding and showing layers becomes an essential technique.

1 To hide a layer, click on the eye icon for the visible layer you want to hide. All objects on the layer are hidden. If you hide the active layer, a red line appears through the Pen icon, indicating that you cannot select or make changes to objects on the layer.

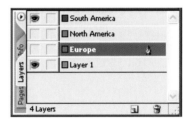

2 To show a hidden layer, click in the empty eye icon box. The eye icon reappears and objects on the layer become visible.

3 To make all layers visible, click the palette menu button (▶); then choose Show All Layers.

4 Hold down Alt/option and click an eye icon to hide all layers except the one on which you click. Hold down Alt/option and click on the same eye icon to show all layers.

5   Drag through the eye icons column to hide or show a continuous sequence of layers. Start dragging on an eye icon to hide the layers you drag through. Start dragging on an empty eye box to show the layers you drag through.

Locking Layers

Use the column between the eye icon column and the layer names to control the lock/unlock status of a layer. When you lock a layer you cannot select or edit objects on that layer, but the layer remains visible. As a document becomes more and more complex, lock layers to avoid accidentally moving or editing objects on those layers.

1   To lock a layer, click in the empty lock column next to the layer you want to lock. A pencil with a red line through it (the lock symbol) appears. If you lock the active layer, a red line also appears through the Pen icon.

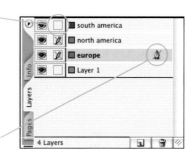

2   To unlock a layer, click the lock symbol. The lock column becomes empty. To unlock all layers, choose Unlock All Layers from the Layers palette menu.

3   Hold down Alt/option and click the lock box to lock all layers except the one on which you click. Hold down Alt/option and click on the same lock box to unlock all layers.

4   Drag through the lock box column to lock or unlock a continuous sequence of layers. Start dragging on an empty lock box to lock the layers you drag through. Start dragging on a lock symbol to unlock the layers you drag through.

Grouping Objects

Group separate objects together so that they work as one single unit. Groups are useful when you want to fix the position of particular objects relative to one another. You can move and transform groups without changing the relative position of the individual objects within the group. You can group two or more groups to form a nested hierarchy.

When you group selected objects that are initially on different layers, they become a group on the layer that contained the frontmost of the selected objects.

1 To group objects, make sure that you have two or more objects selected. (See pages 34–35 for techniques for selecting multiple objects.)

2 Choose Object>Group (Ctrl/Command+G). The objects become a group, and a selection bounding box with eight handles appears defining the perimeter of the group.

The default keyboard shortcut for ungrouping a group is Ctrl/Command+Shift+G.

3 To ungroup objects, select the group using the Selection tool. Choose Object>Ungroup. (If the Ungroup command is dimmed, you have not selected a group.) The objects are ungrouped, but all of them remain individually selected. If you want to make changes to an individual object, click on some empty space to deselect the objects, and then reselect the object you want to work on.

Working with Groups

Once you have grouped objects, you can move, scale and transform the group as a single unit. You can also work on individual elements within groups.

Moving Groups

1. To move a group, select it with the Selection tool. A bounding box appears around the perimeter of the grouped objects. Position your cursor on one of the grouped objects, and then press and drag to reposition the group.

2. Hold down Shift and then press and drag an object in the group to constrain the move to vertical, horizontal or 45-degree increments.

3. Hold down Alt/option and then press and drag an object in the group to make a copy of the group.

To lock an object or group so that it cannot be accidentally moved, transformed or deleted, select the object using the Selection tool, and then choose Object>Lock Position. You can select a locked object or group, but if you try to drag it, the cursor changes to a padlock to indicate the locked status:

To unlock a selected locked object or group, choose Object>Unlock Position.

4. You can also position groups with numeric precision using the X and Y entry fields in the Control or Transform palettes. Remember to select a Reference point in the palette to specify the exact point of the group you want to position. (See pages 36–37 for more information on positioning objects.)

Manually Resizing Groups

1. To manually resize a group, select one of the grouped objects using the Selection tool. Press and drag on a handle to change the size of all objects in the group. This does not change type size for any text objects in the group.

2 Hold down Shift, and press and drag a selection handle to scale objects in the group in proportion. This does not change type size for any text objects in the group.

3 Hold down Ctrl/ Command+Shift and press and drag a selection handle to scale objects and their contents (type or image) in proportion.

Using the Direct Selection Tool with Groups

You can use the Direct Selection tool to reposition objects within the group, to delete objects from a group and to edit individual objects without having to first ungroup the group.

1 Select the Direct Selection tool. Click on an object within the group. The object is highlighted as an editable shape. Continue working with the Direct Selection tool to make changes to the selected path. (For further information on working with objects using the Direct Selection tool, see Chapter 16.)

To avoid editing the shape of an open path as you reposition it, hold down Ctrl/ Command, and drag the path.

2 To reposition an object within the group, select the Direct Selection tool, click on an object in the group to select it, and drag the object. You can hold down Shift, and click on additional objects to select more than one object within the group.

3 To delete an object from a group, select it with the Direct Selection tool; then press the Backspace or Delete key, or choose Edit>Clear.

The Group Selection Tool

The Group Selection tool allows you to work efficiently with groups that have been nested within other groups to form a hierarchy. The Group Selection tool is not a tool in its own right. With the Direct Selection tool selected, if you hold down the Alt/ option key, the Direct Selection tool becomes the Group Selection tool, indicated by an additional "+" symbol at the cursor.

1   To select objects within nested groups with the Group Selection tool, first select the Direct Selection tool. Hold down Alt/option on the keyboard. A "+" symbol appears with the tool cursor. Click on an object that is part of a group to select a single object only.

2   Still with the Alt/option key held down, click a second time on the same object. This selects any objects that are grouped with the first object you clicked on. You could now recolor the selected objects, delete them, and so on.

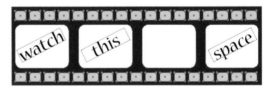

3   Alt/option+click a third time on the same object to select any other groups that are grouped with the group already selected. Continue to Alt/option+click on the same object to progressively select outward through the grouping hierarchy.

Aligning Objects

Alignment is one of the underlying principles of good design. The Align palette provides controls for aligning objects relative to each other vertically and/or horizontally. The top row of icons in the Align palette controls vertical and horizontal alignment.

1 To align objects, use the Selection tool to select two or more objects. Make sure the Align palette is showing by choosing Window>Align (Shift+F7) if it is not.

2 Click one of the Horizontal Align buttons to align objects along their left or right edges or horizontal centers. Objects align to the leftmost or rightmost object if you choose Align left/right edges. Objects align along the horizontal center point of the selected objects if you choose Align horizontal centers.

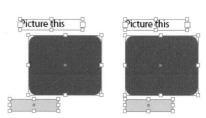

3 Click one of the Vertical Align buttons to align objects along their top or bottom edges or vertical centers. Objects align to the topmost or bottommost object if you choose Align top/bottom edges. Objects align along the vertical center point of the selected objects if you choose Align vertical centers.

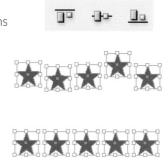

Distributing Objects

To create equal space between objects or equal distance between the lefts, rights, tops or bottoms of selected objects, you can use the Distribute buttons in the second row of the Align palette.

The Distribute options work only when you have three or more objects selected.

To distribute objects, select three or more objects using the Selection tool.

Select the Use Spacing option and enter a spacing value before you click on one of the Distribute Objects buttons to create a specific amount of space between the edges or centers you specify:

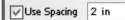

2 Click one of the Horizontal Distribute buttons to space objects so that the distance from left edge to left edge, right edge to right edge, or horizontal center to horizontal center is equal.

3 Click one of the Vertical Distribute buttons to space objects so that the distance from top edge to top edge, bottom edge to bottom edge, or vertical center to vertical center is equal.

Distributing Space Equally Between Objects

Rather than spacing objects with equal amounts of space between specific parts of the selected objects, you can create equal amounts of space between each object.

Select the Use Spacing option and enter a spacing value before you click one of the Distribute Spacing buttons to create an equal amount of space between the selected objects:

Choose Show Options from the Align palette menu (▶). Two additional buttons appear at the bottom of the palette. Select three or more objects. Click the Distribute vertical/horizontal space button to create equal amounts of space vertically or horizontally between the selected objects.

Anchored Objects

Anchored objects can be text or graphic frames which are attached to a specific point in text. When the text reflows, the anchored object moves, maintaining its position relative to the point in the text to which it is anchored. The exact position of the anchored object is determined by settings you create in the Anchored Object Options dialog box.

Inline Anchored Objects

Inline anchored objects are useful when you want to include a small graphic in the middle of text, like this: , and also for larger objects at the start of a paragraph as in the following example.

1   To set up an Inline anchored object, start by creating the object you want to anchor and scaling it to the size at which you want to use it. Choose Edit>Cut to place the object on the clipboard.

2   Select the Type tool; then click in the text to place the Text Insertion Point where you want to insert the anchored object.

3   Choose Edit>Paste to insert the anchored object at the insertion point. Depending on the size of the object, it may obscure surrounding text.

arket performance
    The result of the regional aviation boom is that the market value of such carriers has grown at a compound annual rate of 22%. Regional service has become the cornerstone of several recovery plans.

To view the anchor point marker (¥) in text, choose Type>Show Hidden Characters if they are not already showing.

4   To control the positioning of the object, select it using the Selection tool, and then choose Object>Anchored Object>Options.

With the Inline radio button selected, use the Y Offset entry

Before you convert a frame into an anchored object, scale it to the required size. It is easier to scale and manipulate text and graphic frames when they are not affected by the constraints of being an anchored object.

box to control the vertical positioning of the anchored object. Use a negative value to move the object downward.

5 Apply Text Wrap to the object, if necessary, to control the space between the object and the surrounding text.

Stagnant market performance

The result of the regional aviation boom is that the market value of such carriers has grown at a compound annual rate of 22%. Regional service has become the cornerstone of several recovery plans.

Stagnant market performance

The result of the regional aviation boom is that the market value of such carriers has grown at a compound annual rate of 22%. Regional service has become the cornerstone of several recovery plans.

Above Line Anchored Objects

Above Line anchored objects can be useful when you want an object to behave like a paragraph element and to flow with text.

In the Anchored Object Options dialog box, select Custom from the Position pop-up menu to access advanced controls for creating anchored objects.

1 To create an Above Line anchored object, follow steps 1–3 above.

2 Select the anchored object, then choose Object>Anchored Object>Options. Select the Above Line radio button. Use the Alignment pop-up menu to choose a standard alignment for the object.

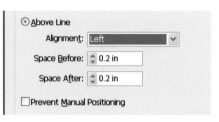

In the Anchored Object Options dialog box, select the Prevent Manual Positioning checkbox to disallow any manual adjustments to the object using the Selection tool.

3 Enter values for Space Before/Space After to control the amount of space above and below the object.

Stagnant market performance

The result of the regional aviation boom is that the market value of such carriers has grown at a compound annual rate of 22%. Regional service has become the cornerstone of several recovery plans.

Working with Color

Color adds impact to publications, from the simplest of marketing leaflets through to glossy magazines. Techniques for handling and applying color will quickly become an important part of your work in InDesign. This chapter shows you how to create, apply and manage color in your documents, using the Color tools in the Toolbox, the Color palette, the Swatches palette and the Gradient palette.

Covers

Chapter Eight

Filling and Stroking Objects

Using the Fill and Stroke boxes, in conjunction with the Swatches palette, you can apply a fill and/or stroke color to a basic shape (such as a rectangle or circle), a text or graphic frame, or a path created with the Pen or Pencil tool.

When you create a shape, such as a closed path, a rectangle, a circle or a polygon, it is automatically filled with the currently selected fill color, and its path is stroked or outlined with the currently set stroke color and weight.

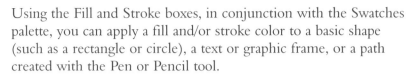

1 To apply a fill color to a selected object or frame, click on the Fill box to make it active. Click on a color swatch in the Swatches palette. (Choose Window>Swatches if the Swatches palette is not showing.) The color is applied to the selected object.

2 To apply a stroke color to a selected object or frame, click on the Stroke box to make it active. Click on a color swatch in the Swatches palette. The color is applied as a stroke to the path of the selected object.

3 Changing the fill and/or stroke color for a selected object does not change the default fill/stroke color. The default fill color for basic shapes is None with a 1 point black stroke. To set a default fill/stroke color for objects, make sure nothing is selected, click the Fill or Stroke box to select it, and then click on a color in the Swatches palette. The Fill/Stroke box changes to reflect the color swatch you clicked on. Any basic shapes, or paths drawn with the Pen or Pencil tool, are automatically filled/stroked with the new default fill/stroke color.

When you draw an open path with the Pen or Pencil tool, if there is a fill color selected, InDesign attempts to fill the path along an imaginary line from one end point to the other. This can be disconcerting at first. Click the Fill box and then click the None button to prevent this happening.

4 To apply a fill or stroke of None to a selected object, path or frame, make sure either the Fill or Stroke box is selected as required; then click the None button. A red line through the Fill or Stroke box indicates a fill or stroke of None. Objects with a fill of None are transparent. You can also click on the None button in the Swatches palette or in the bottom-left corner of the Color palette.

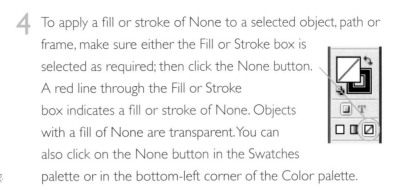

Keyboard shortcuts such as "D" and "X" work only if you do not have the Text insertion point active in a text frame.

5 Click the Swap arrow to swap the fill and stroke colors for a selected object, or hold down Shift and press X on the keyboard.

6 To apply a default fill of None and a black stroke to a selected object, click the Default Fill and Stroke button below the Fill box in the Toolbox, or press D on the keyboard.

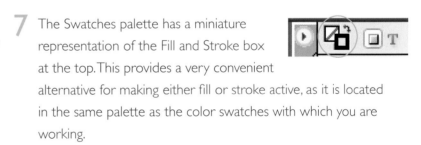

Be careful when you have a text frame selected with the Selection tool and you are applying color. Make sure you have the correct Formatting Affects Container/Text button selected, depending on what you want to color.

7 The Swatches palette has a miniature representation of the Fill and Stroke box at the top. This provides a very convenient alternative for making either fill or stroke active, as it is located in the same palette as the color swatches with which you are working.

The Formatting Affects Container/ Text buttons appear in the Toolbox below the Fill and Stroke boxes, at the top of the Swatches palette and on the left of the Color palette.

8 When you are working with a text frame, selected with the Selection tool, you can select the Formatting Affects Container button if you want to color the frame's background or stroke. Select the Formatting Affects Text button if you want to color the type inside the frame. You also need to make sure that you select the fill or stroke box as required.

The Swatches Palette

Use the Swatches palette to create a palette of colors you want to use consistently throughout a document. The colors you create and store in the Swatches palette are saved with the document.

The Swatches palette consists initially of a set of default swatches. You cannot make changes to [None], [Black] or [Registration]. You cannot delete [None], [Paper] or [Registration].

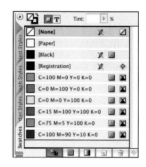

Viewing Swatches

1 To show the Swatches palette, choose Window>Swatches, or click the Swatches tab if the palette is docked in the Palette bar. Click one of the swatches buttons at the bottom of the Swatches palette to control which types of swatches are visible in the palette. You can choose All Swatches, Color Swatches or Gradient Swatches.

2 The color model used to create a color is indicated in the rightmost column of the Swatches palette. The CMYK quarters icon indicates that the color is in CMYK mode. Three bars (red, green, blue) indicate that the color is an RGB color.

3 A grey box to the left of the color model box indicates a process color – a color that will be separated into its cyan, magenta, yellow and black components when the page is color separated at output. A grey circle to the left of the color model box indicates a spot color – a color that will create its own plate when printing separations.

Add, Delete and Edit Swatches

A spot color is printed with a premixed ink on a printing press. At 100% (i.e., no tint), a spot color is printed as a solid color and has no dot pattern. Spot colors create their own, separate plate when you print separations.

A process color is printed using the four process inks – Cyan, Magenta, Yellow and blacK (CMYK).

RGB color mode is most useful when you are creating publications that will be printed in-house as color composites, or for publications intended for the World Wide Web.

Leave the Name with Color Value option selected for InDesign to automatically name the color with the exact color breakdown you define. Switch off the option and enter a name if you want to name the color yourself.

Select Unnamed Swatch to leave objects in the document already filled or stroked with the color you are deleting filled or stroked with that color. The color will no longer appear in the Swatches palette as a "named" swatch.

Use the Swatches palette to create new process and spot colors, to convert spot colors to process and vice versa, to delete colors, and to create tints and gradients.

Creating New Color Swatches

1 Choose New Color Swatch from the Swatches palette menu (▶). Enter a name for the color. Choose either Spot or Process from the Color Type pop-up. Choose one of CMYK, RGB or LAB from the Color Mode pop-up, depending on your output requirements.

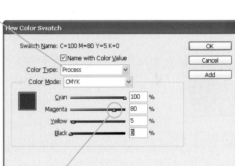

2 Drag the color slider triangles or enter values in the % entry fields. If you have an object selected when you create a new color swatch, the new color is applied to either its fill or its stroke, depending on whether the Fill or Stroke box is active in the Toolbox. If no object is selected when you create a new color, it becomes the new default color for fill or stroke, again depending on which box is active.

Deleting Swatches from the Swatches Palette

To remove a swatch from the Swatches palette, click on it to select it, and then click the Wastebasket button. Alternatively, drag the swatch onto the Wastebasket. In the Delete Swatch dialog box, use the Defined Swatch pop-up to choose a color (from the remaining colors) that will be used to replace instances of the color you are deleting.

To convert a color from Spot to Process or vice versa, double-click the swatch, and then use the Color Type pop-up to change from one type to the other:

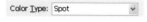

Color Type: Spot

If you do not have anything selected when you edit a swatch, all objects to which the color was previously applied are updated, and the edited color becomes the default fill or stroke color, depending on which color box is active in the Toolbox.

Tints of a spot color print on the same separations plate as the spot color. A tint of a process color multiplies each of the CMYK process inks by the tint percentage. For example, a 50% tint of C=0 M=40 Y=100 K=10 creates a tint color of C=0 M=20 Y=50 K=5.

Editing Existing Colors

1 Click on the color swatch to select it, and then choose Swatch Options from the Swatches palette menu (▶); alternatively double-click the swatch you want to edit.

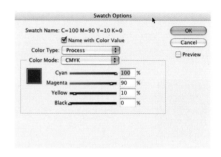

2 Use the Swatch Options dialog box to make changes to the color. Select the Preview option to see the changes implemented in the document before you OK the dialog box. Click OK when you are satisfied. If you have an object selected when you edit a color swatch, the fill or stroke of the object will change to reflect the change made to the color. All other objects to which the color has been previously applied will also update accordingly.

Creating Tints

You can create tints of existing spot or process colors using the Swatches palette menu.

1 To create a tint, click on a color in the Swatches palette to set the base color for the tint. Choose New Tint Swatch from the Swatches palette menu. Drag the Tint slider, or enter a percentage value to define the tint. OK the dialog box. The tint appears in the Swatches palette with the same name as the original base color, but with the tint % value also indicated.

2 If you edit a color that is also the base color for a tint, the tint is adjusted accordingly.

The Color Palette

To show the Color palette choose Window>Color, or click the Color tab if the palette is docked in the Palette bar, or use the keyboard shortcut F6.

The Swatches palette is the primary palette for creating and editing colors in Adobe InDesign. You can also mix colors in the Color palette and then save the color as a swatch, so that it becomes a "named" color.

1   The Color palette initially appears with the Tint slider visible, and reflects the color currently selected in the Swatches palette. To create a color in the Color palette, click either the Fill or the Stroke box; then choose a color model from the palette menu.

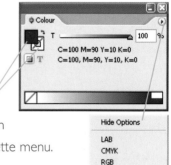

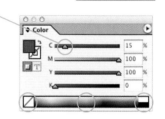

If you select an object and then edit its fill or stroke color in the Color palette, the change is only applied to the selected object; the change does not affect other objects to which the original color is applied.

2   Either drag the color component sliders or enter values in the entry fields. Alternatively, you can select None, Black or White, or click in the color spectrum bar at the bottom of the palette.

If you select an object that is filled or stroked with a color from the Swatches palette, the Color palette displays the Tint slider.

3   To save a color created in the Color palette, click the New Swatch button (▣) in the Swatches palette, or choose Add to Swatches from the Color palette menu. The color becomes a swatch in the Swatches palette and is a now a named color. The Color palette displays the Tint slider for the color, as it is now a swatch.

A "named" color is a color that appears in the Swatches palette. As such, it is saved with the document and can be used repeatedly and consistently. Choose Add Unnamed Colors from the Swatches palette menu to create named swatches for all unnamed colors in the document.

4   A "named" color is a color that has an entry in the Swatches palette. An "unnamed" color is one that you have created using the Color palette, and possibly applied to an object in your document, but that does not appear in the Swatches palette. It is easier to identify, edit and manage colors if they appear as named colors in the Swatches palette. Creating named colors from the outset is a good habit to get into.

Color Matching Systems

Color Matching Systems such as PANTONE®, FOCOLTONE® and TRUMATCH™ are necessary when you want to reproduce colors accurately, especially colors in logos, which need to be reproduced consistently. You can choose predefined colors from a number of color matching systems.

The Web color library helps guarantee consistent color results on both Windows and Macintosh platforms. The Web palette consists of the 216 RGB colors most commonly used by web browsers to display 8-bit images.

1 To choose a color from a color matching system, such as PANTONE, show the Swatches palette. Choose New Swatch from the palette menu (▶).

2 In the New Color Swatch dialog box, select a color matching system from the Color Mode pop-up menu.

3 Either scroll through the PANTONE list, or, to access a color swatch quickly, type the number of the PANTONE color you want to

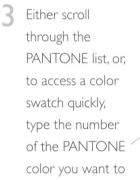

select into the PANTONE box. Click OK to add the color to the Swatches palette.

4 To convert an existing PANTONE color to its CMYK equivalent, click on the color to select it, and then choose Swatch Options from the Swatches palette menu. Alternatively, you can double-click the PANTONE entry in the Swatches palette. Use the Color Model pop-up menu to change the setting to CMYK, and then use the Color Type pop-up menu to change the setting to Process.

You can identify spot colors in the Swatches palette by the Spot Color icon that appears to the right of the spot color entry in the Swatches palette:

Creating and Applying Gradients

A gradient is a gradual transition from one color to another color. Gradients can be linear or radial. You can fill objects and frames with a gradient fill, and they can be applied to strokes and also to text – without first having to convert the text to paths.

To add additional colors to a gradient, position your cursor just below the gradient ramp, and then click to add another color stop. Apply color to additional stops in the same way that you apply color to the Start and End stops:

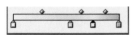

To remove an additional color stop, drag it off the gradient ramp.

1 To create a gradient, choose New Gradient Swatch from the Swatches palette menu ( ). Enter a name for the gradient. Use the Type pop-up to choose between Linear and Radial. To specify the start and end colors for the gradient, click on either of the "stop" icons on the Gradient Ramp. The triangle on the top of the stop becomes highlighted to indicate that it is selected.

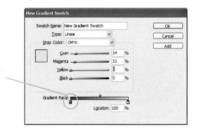

2 Choose a color model from the Stop Color pop-up menu. Enter CMYK values, or drag the sliders to mix a color. Click on the other stop icon and repeat the process.

When you work with the Gradient palette, make sure that the Swatches palette is visible, so that you can choose start and end colors for the gradient.

3 Drag the diamond icon along the top of the Gradient Ramp to control the point at which both colors in the gradient are at 50%. Click OK when you are satisfied with the settings. The gradient is added to the Swatches palette.

Click the Reverse button if you want the gradient to flow in the opposite direction:

The Gradient Palette

You can also use the Gradient palette to create a gradient.

1 Choose Window>Gradient to show the Gradient palette, or click the Gradient tab if the palette is docked in the Palette bar. Choose from Linear or Radial in the Type pop-up.

Drag the diamond icon along the top of the Gradient Ramp to specify the midpoints of the gradient, or click on the diamond and then enter a value in the Location entry field.

2 To specify the start and end colors for the gradient, click on either of the "Stop" icons on the Gradient Ramp. The triangle on the top of the stop becomes highlighted to indicate that it is selected. Hold down Alt/option, and click on an existing color in the Swatches palette. Repeat this process for the other stop.

3 Enter an angle for the gradient in the Angle entry field.

4 Click the New Swatch button (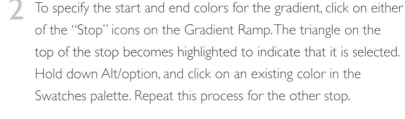) in the Swatches palette to add the gradient swatch to the Swatches palette.

*To apply a gradient to text, either select the text with the Type tool, or select a text frame with the Selection tool, but make sure that you also select the Formatting Affects Text button (**T**) in the Toolbox or the Swatches palette. Click on a gradient swatch, or click the Apply Gradient button:*

GRADIENT

Applying Gradients

Once you have saved a gradient in the Swatches palette, you can apply it to objects, frames, strokes and text.

1 To apply a gradient fill, select an object or frame. Click the Fill box in the Toolbox to make it active. Then click on a Gradient fill swatch in the Swatches palette. Alternatively, click the Apply Gradient button below the Fill/Stroke boxes in the Toolbox. This applies either the default Black/White gradient, or the most recently selected gradient.

Radial gradients start from the center and work outwards.

Hold down Shift as you drag with the gradient tool to constrain the angle of the gradient to multiples of 45 degrees.

2 The Gradient tool allows you to control the angle and length of a gradient. Make sure you select an object with a gradient applied to it. Select the Gradient tool. Position your cursor on the gradient object, then press and drag. As you do so you will see a line. The line determines the direction and length of the gradient. For a linear gradient, the start and end colors fill any part of the object you do not drag the line across. For radial gradients, the end color fills any part of the object you do not drag the line across.

Managing and Editing Text

The Check Spelling dialog box, together with the Find and Replace dialog box, are two powerful tools that help you work quickly and effectively with text files in your documents. This chapter also covers type on paths, as well as text wrap, which is vitally important when you want to control the space between text and the edge of images on your page.

Covers

Chapter Nine

Spell Checking

Before you begin spell checking, make sure the correct language is selected – choose Edit>Preferences>Dictionary (Windows), or InDesign>Preferences>Dictionary (Mac); then choose the correct language from the Language pop-up.

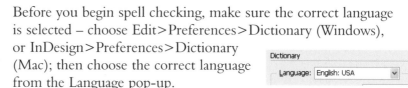

1   To check spelling in a document, select the Type tool, and then either highlight a range of text, or click into a text frame to place the Text insertion point. Choose Edit>Check Spelling.

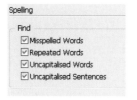
2   Choose an option from the Search pop-up to define the scope of the spell check, and click the Start button. InDesign highlights the first word not in its spell check dictionary. The unrecognized word appears in the Not in Dictionary field and in the Change to field. InDesign lists possible correct spellings in the Suggested Corrections list box.

3   To replace the incorrect word with a suggestion from the list, click on a suggested word, and then click the Change button. InDesign substitutes the correction in the text and moves on to the next unrecognized word. Click the Change All button to change every instance of the same spelling error. To accept the spelling of an unrecognized word as correct, click the Ignore button. Click the Ignore All button if there are multiple instances of the word in the story.

4   Click the Done button to finish spell checking, either when InDesign has checked the entire story, or at any time during spell checking.

Adding Words to the Dictionary

Use Edit> Preferences> Dictionary (Windows), or InDesign> Preferences>Dictionary (Mac), to specify whether the text-composition engine composes text using the word list from the user dictionary, the document's internal dictionary, or both.

You can add words that InDesign does not recognise to the selected dictionary. This is particularly useful if you regularly use specialist or technical words in your documents.

1 To add a word to the dictionary, first start a spell check. When InDesign identifies a word not in the dictionary that you want to add, click the Add button.

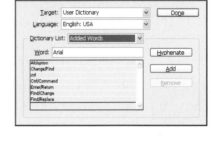

2 Select User Dictionary as the target dictionary to store hyphenation and spelling exceptions in a dictionary file that resides on the hard disk of your computer. Select the document name from the Target pop-up menu to store spelling and hyphenation exceptions inside the document.

You can override InDesign's suggestions by inserting your own tilde marks.

Enter one, two, or three tilde marks to rank hyphenation points. One tilde mark indicates your preferred choice. Three tilde marks represents your least preferred choice. Enter the same number of tilde marks to indicate equal ranking.

To prevent all instances of a word from hyphenating, enter a tilde mark in front of the word.

3 Click the Hyphenate button to see InDesign's suggested hyphenation breaks, indicated by tilde marks (~).

Word: be~~z~ier   [Hyphenate]

4 Click the Add button to add the word to the dictionary. The word appears in the list box with its hyphenation points indicated. To remove a word from the list of added words, click on a word in the list and then click the Remove button. Click Done when you finish adding words.

Edit Dictionary Command

You can use the Edit Dictionary command to add and remove words at any time as you work on your document.

Customized user dictionaries are stored in a file with a .udc or .not extension. These files can be copied from system to system if it is important, in a workgroup situation, for every member to have the same dictionary file on their system in order to ensure consistency.

1 To add or remove a word, choose Edit> Dictionary. Use the techniques listed in steps 2–4 above. Click the Done button when you finish editing the dictionary.

Find/Change Words

Use the pop-up to the right of the Find What and Change To entry fields to search for, or replace with, special characters.

The Find/Change dialog box allows you to find particular words or phrases in a story or document and then change them to something else. For example, you could change misspelling of a technical word throughout a story or an entire publication.

1. To find and change one word or phrase to another word or phrase, select the Type tool. Click into a text frame to place the Text insertion point. Choose Edit>Find/Change. Enter the word or phrase you want to search for in the Find What entry field. Enter the text you want to change to in the Change To entry field. Use the Search pop-up to specify the scope of the Find/Replace routine.

Once you have entered a word or phrase in the Find What entry field, you can click the Done button, and then choose Edit>Find Next (Ctrl/Command+Alt/option+F) to move to occurrences of the Find What text.

2. Select Whole Word to ensure that InDesign finds only instances of complete words. For example, if you search for "as", select the Whole Word option so that the search does not find instances of the a+s character pair in words such as "was" and "class".

Select the Case Sensitive option when you want to find text that matches exactly the capitalization used in the Find What field. For example, if you entered "InDesign" with the Case Sensitive option selected, the search would not find "indesign", or "Indesign". Also, when you use the Case Sensitive option, the text you change to matches the exact capitalization of the text in the Change To field.

3. When you have made the appropriate selections and entered the find and change text, click the Find Next button. InDesign moves to the first instance of the find text and highlights it, scrolling the document window if necessary to show the highlighted word. Click the Change button to change that instance only. Click the Find Next button to continue the search.

4. Click the Change/Find button to change the highlighted text and move to the next instance. Click the Change All button to change every instance of the Find What text. A Search Complete box indicates how many instances were changed.

Find/Change Basic Text Formatting

You can also use the Find/Change dialog box to search for instances of formatting attributes, such as a particular font, size or style, and then change these attributes to something different.

1 To search for text formatting attributes, select the Type tool, and click into a text frame to place the Text insertion point, or highlight a range of text if you want to limit the operation to specific text.

2 Choose Edit>Find/ Change. Use the Search pop-up to define the extent of the Find/ Change routine. Do not enter any text in the Find What/Change To entry fields. Click the More options button (which becomes Fewer options).

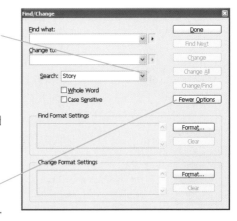

There are Find/Change capabilities for virtually all character and paragraph formatting attributes. Click the various categories in the Find Format Settings dialog box to explore the possibilities.

3 Click the Format button in the Find Format Settings area. Select a category from the categories list box, and then select

the attributes you want to find. Make sure you specify exactly the attributes you want to search for. If you leave a field blank, this indicates to InDesign that the attribute is not relevant to your search. For example, if you want to find instances of Arial Bold in a story, you can leave the Size entry field blank; InDesign will then find any instance of Arial Bold, regardless of its size. Enter a size value only if you want to limit the search to a particular character size.

Be logical and patient when finding and changing complex sets of attributes. It is easy to accidentally specify an attribute that does not exist in your publication, and consequently get the message that no instances were found.

4 OK the dialog box when you are satisfied with the settings. The settings you have chosen are indicated in the Find Style Settings list box.

The more values you enter, and/or options you choose, the more limited the search becomes.

5 Click the Format button in the Change Format Settings area. Select a category from the Categories list box, and select

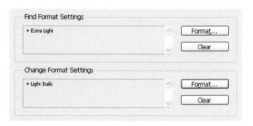

the formatting attributes you want to change to. Make sure you specify exactly the attributes you want. OK the dialog box when you are satisfied. The settings you chose are indicated in the Change Format Settings readout box. When you specify Formats, warning triangles appear next to the Find What/Change To fields to indicate that formatting settings are in force. These are especially useful if you have clicked the Fewer Options button

Typically, when things go wrong with a Find/Change it is because the attributes you specify for the search do not exist in the document. Go back out of the Find/Change dialog box and check that you know exactly what you are looking for by checking actual settings on text in the story.

to condense the palette, as unnecessary format settings can cause simple Find/Change operations to go wrong.

6 When you no longer need your Format settings, click the Clear buttons in the Format Settings areas to revert all Find/Change settings to their default values. If you are having problems getting a particular Find/Change routine to work, it is sometimes useful to use the Clear button to reset everything, and then set up your Find/Change criteria from scratch.

7 Use the Find Next, Change, Change All and Change/Find buttons to proceed with the search and replace.

Text Wrap

Controlling Text Wrap becomes necessary when you start to combine text frames and graphic frames on a page, particularly when they overlap each other.

1. To wrap text around a graphic frame, select the graphic frame using the Selection tool. It doesn't matter whether the picture frame is in front of or behind the text frame.

2. Choose Window>Text & Tables>Text Wrap (Ctrl/Command+Alt/option+W) to show the Text Wrap palette. Click the Wrap Around Bounding Box button to wrap text around all sides of the graphic frame.

If you no longer need text wrap settings on an object, make sure it is selected, and then click the No Wrap button in the Text Wrap palette:

3. Enter values for Top, Bottom, Left and Right offsets to control how far text is pushed away from the various edges of the frame. Press Enter/Return to apply changes. When you select the frame with the Selection tool, a faint blue standoff border, with hollow corner handles, appears around the frame to visually indicate the text wrap area (provided the frame edges are visible).

4. Click the Jump Object button to prevent text flowing on either side of the picture frame. When you choose this option you can control only the Top and Bottom offset amounts.

5 Click the Jump to Next Column button to prevent text from flowing either side of the frame and after it. Text is forced to the top of the next column. Beware that, in a single column text frame, where text is not threaded to another frame, this option forces text after the frame into overmatter.

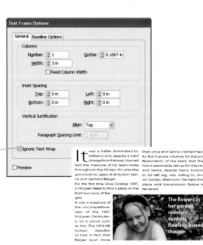

6 You can also apply text wrap to a selected text frame. This can be useful for such things as pull quotes, where text frames overlap other text frames.

Text Wrap and Stacking Order

When you place a text frame over an image that has text wrap applied to it, some or all of the text may disappear from the frame. This is caused by the text wrap setting, which affects text in frames both behind and in front of it. Use the following technique to prevent this happening on an individual text frame.

If you prefer text wrap settings to affect only text in frames below the graphic frame in the stacking order, choose Edit>Preferences> Composition (Windows), or InDesign> Preferences>Composition (Mac); then select the Text Wrap Only Affects Text Beneath option:

> Text Wrap
> ☐ Justify Text Next to an Object
> ☑ Skip By Leading
> ☐ Text Wrap Only Affects Text Beneath

This is the text wrap behavior with which QuarkXPress users are most familiar.

Select the text frame using the Selection tool. Choose Object>Text Frame Options (Ctrl/ Command+B). Select the Ignore Text Wrap option. This affects the individual text frame to which you apply the control.

Irregular Text Wrap

As well as wrapping text around rectangular graphic or text frames, you can also wrap text around non-rectangular shape objects such as circles and stars, and along paths created with the Pen or Pencil tool. In addition, you can create text wrap based on a clipping path, or the shape of an imported Adobe Illustrator graphic.

Wrapping Text Around Shapes

To wrap text around a shape frame or a path, choose Window>Type & Tables>Text Wrap (Ctrl/Command+Alt/option+W) to show the Text Wrap palette if it is not already showing. Select the object; then click the Wrap Around Object Shape button. Enter an Offset value. For non-rectangular objects you create a single, standard offset amount – there is only one Offset field available.

See pages 96–98 for information on creating, manipulating and importing images with clipping paths.

Wrapping Text to Clipping Paths

To wrap text around a graphic with a clipping path, make sure you select the image with the Selection tool. Click on the Wrap Around Object Shape button.

2 Choose Show Options from the palette menu, or click the Expand button in the palette tab, to show the extended palette. Choose Same As Clipping from the Type pop-up menu.

To wrap text around an Adobe Illustrator graphic, select Detect Edges from the Type pop-up:

3 Enter a value in the Offset field to control the distance that the text is offset from the image's clipping path.

Type on a Path

You cannot create type on compound paths, such as those created when you use the Pathfinder commands.

Unlike in Illustrator, if a path is stroked with a color before you add type to it, it remains visible when you add the type.

If you enter too much text, the additional text becomes overmatter. To see all the text, either thread the text onto another path or into another frame, or reduce the type size.

You can flip type manually by dragging the center bracket across the path, or by selecting the Flip checkbox in the Type on a Path Options dialog box.

You often need to use Baseline Shift and Kerning/ Tracking settings to fine-tune the final effect for type on a path.

Running type along a path can produce interesting and unusual results. You can apply type to open and closed paths, including shapes or frames.

1 To apply type to a path, select the Type on a Path tool. Position your cursor on a path. The path does not need to be selected, but make sure you see the additional "+" symbol appear on the cursor ( ), which indicates that the text will be applied to the path.

2 Click on the path. A Text insertion point appears on the path. Enter type using the keyboard. You can enter type along the entire length of the path.

3 When you select the text with a Selection tool, the In and Out ports appear at the start and end of the path. On the inside of the ports are the start and end brackets. Drag the start or end bracket to adjust the length of the text area on the path. In the middle of the path is the path type center bracket. Drag the center bracket to reposition text along the path after you have adjusted one of the end brackets.

4 To create additional settings for type on a path, with the path type selected, choose Type>Type on a Path>Options. Use the Align and To Path pop-ups to specify which part of the type aligns to which part of the path. In this example, the ascenders of the type align to the bottom of the path. Use the Spacing control to compensate, if necessary, for the way in which characters fan out on some curves.

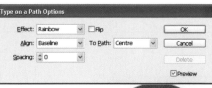

The Pages Palette and Master Pages

The Pages palette provides key functionality for adding and deleting document pages and for building Master pages, as well as for navigating from page to page in a multi-page document.

Master pages bring consistency to the repeating elements in documents consisting of more than a few pages. Typical master page elements include automatic page numbering, date lines, headers and footers, and often graphic elements such as rules and color boxes. You can also specify columns on the master page.

Covers

Chapter Ten

The Pages Palette

Use the Pages palette to move from page to page, to move to master pages, and to add and delete both document pages and master pages. Click the Pages tab if the palette is docked in the Palette bar, or choose Window>Pages (F12) to show the palette.

When working in the Pages palette, an initial distinction needs to be made concerning the way in which you select a spread or page on which to work. In InDesign you can "select" or "target" a spread or page.

Choose Palette Options from the Pages palette menu to access the Palette Options dialog box:

This dialog box allows you to control the arrangement and size of page icons in the Pages palette. You can choose options to show page icons vertically, and to control the size of the page icons. You can also control whether master pages or document pages appear at the top of the palette.

Selecting Spreads/Pages

Select a page or spread when you want to change settings such as margin and column settings and guides on a particular spread – in other words settings that affect the page rather than objects on the page. This is most important when there are multiple pages displayed at a low level of magnification in the document window. Selecting a spread ensures that the changes you make affect the page you intend them to affect. A selected page is indicated by a highlighted page icon, not highlighted page numbers.

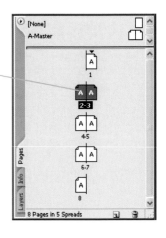

To select a page, click once on the page icon in the Pages palette. To select a spread, click once on the page numbers below the spread icons.

A spread normally consists of two pages viewed side by side as, for example, in a magazine or this book.

2 Double-click a page icon to select and target it. The page or spread is centered in the document window.

Targeting Spreads/Pages

Target a page or spread when you want to make changes to objects on a particular spread or page. For example, when more than one spread is visible in the document window and you want to paste an object

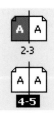

onto a particular spread, make sure you target it before you paste the object. A "targeted" page or spread is indicated by a highlighted page number, as opposed to a highlighted page icon.

1 Working on, selecting, or modifying an object on a page automatically activates the page or spread as the target page or spread.

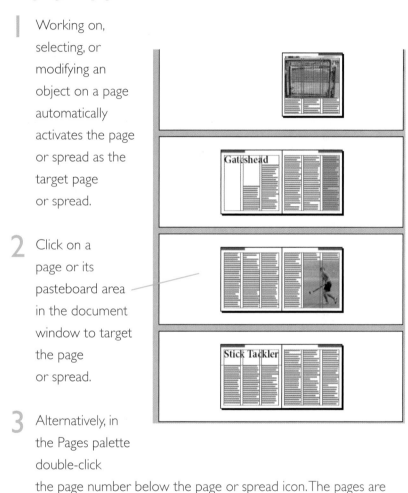

2 Click on a page or its pasteboard area in the document window to target the page or spread.

3 Alternatively, in the Pages palette double-click the page number below the page or spread icon. The pages are centered in the document window.

Inserting and Deleting Pages

To select a consecutive range of pages, select the first page in the range; then hold down Shift and click on the last page to highlight all pages between the two clicks:

You can specify the number of pages in a document in the New Document dialog box, but you can also add and delete pages in the document at any time.

1 To add a page after the currently targeted page or spread – indicated by the highlighted page numbers in the Pages palette – click the New Page button (🔲) in the Pages palette. The new page is automatically based on the same master as the currently targeted page. A master page prefix (which is typically a letter) in the document page icon indicates the master page on which it is based.

2 To insert a single page or multiple pages using the Insert Pages dialog box, choose Insert Pages from the Pages palette menu (▶). Enter the number of pages you want to add. Use the Insert pop-up to specify the placement of the additional pages relative to the page number you specify in the Page Number entry field. In a publication with multiple master pages, choose the master on which the additional pages will be based from the Master pop-up. OK the dialog box.

To select non-consecutive pages, select a page; then hold down Ctrl/Command and click on other pages to add them to the selection:

3 To delete a page, click on the page to select it, and then click the Wastebasket button (or you can drag the page onto the Wastebasket button). You can also choose Delete Page/Spread from the Pages palette menu. OK the warning dialog box.

Moving from Page to Page

There are a number of ways you can move from page to page in a multi-page document. You can use the Pages palette if it is showing, the scroll bars, the Navigator palette, or the page indicator area in the bottom-left corner of the document window.

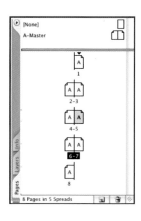

1 To move to another page using the Pages palette, double-click the page icon of the page you want to move to. The page icon you double-click on highlights, as does the page number below it. The page you double-click is centered in the InDesign document window.

Use the keyboard shortcut Ctrl/Command+J to highlight the Page Number entry field; enter a page number, and then press Enter/Return to move to that page.

2 To move to another page using the page indicator area,

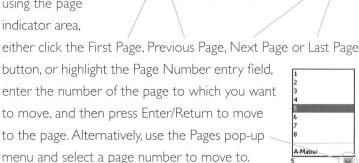

either click the First Page, Previous Page, Next Page or Last Page button, or highlight the Page Number entry field, enter the number of the page to which you want to move, and then press Enter/Return to move to the page. Alternatively, use the Pages pop-up menu and select a page number to move to.

3 To move to other pages, you can use the Up and Down scroll arrows of the publication window to move to different pages or spreads.

4 You can also use the keyboard shortcut, Shift+Page Up/Page Down, to move backward/forward one page at a time.

Repositioning Document Pages

In a multi-page document you can rearrange the order of pages using the Pages palette.

1 To move a page to a new position, position your cursor on the page icon you want to move, and then drag it to a new position within the pages area of the Pages palette. As you drag the page, look for a black vertical bar and the force left/right arrows (which help indicate the position to which the page will move, and the result on surrounding pages, when you release the mouse). Pages throughout the publication are repositioned to make way for the page you move.

To start a facing-pages document with a double-page spread, make sure you have at least three pages in the document, select pages 2 and 3, and then choose Keep Spread Together from the Pages palette menu:

Select and delete page 1. The original pages 2 and 3 become the opening spread for the document:

2 To move a page between two pages in a spread, drag the page icon to the middle of the spread. In a double-sided publication, if you reposition a single page between a spread, provided that Allow Pages to Shuffle is selected in the Pages palette menu (▶), left-hand pages can "shuffle" to become right-hand pages and vice versa. You may need to rearrange objects if your left and right master pages are set up differently.

Insert Pages...
New Master...
Duplicate Spread
Delete Spread
Select Unused Masters

Master Options...
Apply Master to Pages...
Save as Master

Override All Master Page Iten
Remove Selected Local Over
Detach Selection From Maste

Keep Spread Together
✓ Allow Pages to Shuffle

Palette Options...
Numbering & Section Options

Spread Flattening

3 To duplicate a spread or page, drag the page number onto the New Page button (▣) at the bottom of the palette, or select a page/spread and choose Duplicate Spread from the Pages palette menu. When you duplicate a page, all objects on the page are also duplicated. The new pages are added at the end of the document.

Setting Master Pages

Each new document you create has an A-master page by default. All document pages are initially based on the A-Master. When you start a new document, the A-Master settings are determined by the margin and column settings that you specify in the New Document dialog box.

In multi-page documents, position those elements such as automatic page numbering, datelines, headers and footers, and logos that you want to appear on all, or nearly all, of the pages in the document on the master page. When you add pages based on a master page to a document, all the objects on the master page are automatically displayed on the document pages. Master pages are essential for guaranteeing that such objects repeat consistently throughout the document. This is also the most efficient method for placing such repeating objects.

If you edit objects on a master page, these changes are automatically applied to master page objects appearing on all document pages based on that master, provided that you have not edited individual instances of the objects on the document pages.

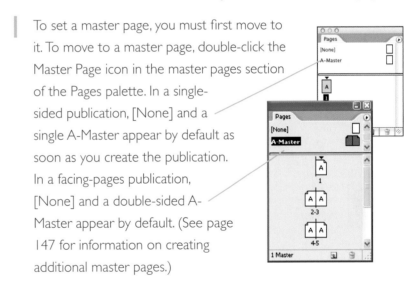

1 To set a master page, you must first move to it. To move to a master page, double-click the Master Page icon in the master pages section of the Pages palette. In a single-sided publication, [None] and a single A-Master appear by default as soon as you create the publication. In a facing-pages publication, [None] and a double-sided A-Master appear by default. (See page 147 for information on creating additional master pages.)

In the New Document dialog box, select the Master Text Frame checkbox to automatically create a text frame on the A-Master page. The master text frame fits within the margins, and has the same number of columns and gutter width as defined in the New Document dialog box.

2 Alternatively, highlight the page indicator field, either by double-clicking in it or by using the keyboard shortcut Ctrl/Command+J, type in the prefix ("A" for an A-Master, "B" for a B-Master, and so on), and then press Enter/Return.

| 25% | | |◀ ◀ A-Master | ▼ | ▶ ▶| ◀ |

3 Create, position and manipulate text, graphic and shape frames, lines and paths on the master as you would on any document page. Objects placed on master pages are initially "locked" on the document pages where they appear. (See page 151 for information on making these master page elements editable.)

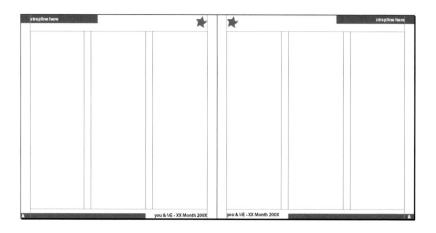

4 When you need to edit objects placed on a master, return to the master page, and then make changes to objects as necessary. Any changes you make are updated on all document pages based on that master.

If you switch on Layout Adjustments and then apply a different master to a document page, the position and size of objects may alter on the document page.

5 Set up ruler guides on a master page if you want them to appear on all publication pages based on that master. Ruler guides that you create on a master page cannot be edited on a document page unless you create a local override on the guide. (See page 151 for information on creating overrides on master page objects.)

Adding and Deleting Master Pages

In some publications you will need more than one set of master pages. For example, in a magazine production environment you might want to have a four- or five-column grid for news pages and a three-column grid for feature pages, while maintaining standard positions for page numbering, date lines and so on. In a book, you might need a different layout grid for the index and front matter, compared to the main body of the book. Use the Pages palette to create additional master pages for a publication.

1 To create a new, blank master, choose New Master from the Pages palette menu (▶). Enter a prefix for the master. A prefix is limited to one character. Enter a name for the master, e.g. "4 col news". Leave the Based on Master pop-up set to None. In the Number of Pages entry field, enter 1 for a single-sided master, or 2 for a double-sided master. OK the dialog box. The new master page appears in the master pages section of the Pages palette and becomes the active page automatically.

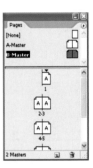

2 You can also hold down Ctrl/Command and then click the New Page button in the Pages palette. If Facing Pages was selected in the New Document dialog box, the new master is a master spread, with left- and right-hand master pages.

3 To create a new master spread from an existing document page or spread, position your cursor on the document page or spread; then drag it into the master pages section of the Pages palette. If the document

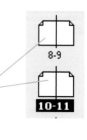

pages you drag into the master pages section are based on a specific master (indicated by the master letter that appears in the page icon), the new master is also based on the same original master page. This in turn is indicated by the master page letter in the new master page icons.

4 To duplicate an existing master page, either drag the master page name (in this example to the left of the master page icons) onto the New Page button ( ), or select the master page name and choose Duplicate Master Spread from the Pages palette menu. This is a useful technique when you want to keep header and footer objects consistent, but need to make some changes, such as implementing a different number of columns. Master pages that you duplicate in this way are replicas of the original master pages, but there is no link between the master page objects on each set of masters. Notice that the new master page icons do not have an A in them.

5 To delete a master page or spread, position your cursor on a master, and then drag it to the Wastebasket button. Alternatively, click on the master name, and then choose Delete Master Spread from the Pages palette menu. OK the Warning dialog box if you want to continue. Any pages to which the master page was applied revert to using [None] as their master.

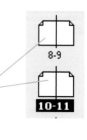

Automatic Page Numbering

Automatic page numbering is useful in multi-page documents that need to have sequential page numbering. Set up automatic page numbering on a master page to automatically number all of the document pages based on that master.

To apply auto page numbering only to individual document pages, move to the document page, and then use the same procedure as for setting auto page numbering on a master page.

1 To set up automatic page numbering, double-click the Master Page icon in the Pages palette. The icon becomes highlighted, indicating that you are now working on the master page. Also, the page indicator in the bottom-left corner of the publication window indicates that you are now working on a master.

2 Create and position a text frame where you want page numbers to appear on all pages based on the current master. (See Chapter 3 for information on creating text frames and entering text.)

Placing the automatic page numbering symbol on a master page guarantees exactly the same positioning and formatting for page numbers throughout a document.

3 Make sure the Text insertion point is flashing in the frame. Choose Type>Insert Special Character>Auto Page Number (Ctrl/Command+Alt/option+N). Alternatively, you can click the right mouse button (Windows), or Control+click the single button (Mac), to access the context-sensitive menu. Choose Insert Special Character> Auto Page Number. An "A" appears in the text frame. This is the automatic page number symbol for A-Master pages.

4 Highlight and format the "A" as you would for any other text character. Add a prefix such as "page" or suffix such as "of 20" as necessary.

5 Move to a document page based on the A-Master to see the automatic page numbers appearing on document pages.

The Allow Pages to Shuffle option in the Pages palette menu controls how pages and spreads are rearranged when you add, remove or section pages in a document.

6 If you are setting up a facing-pages document, remember to set up automatic page numbering on both the left- and right-hand master pages.

Sectioning a document

When you are working with automatic page numbering and you want to change the numbering of a specific range of pages, you can create a section in a document. For example, in a magazine production environment you might want a feature spread to begin on page 28, not page 2.

1 To change page numbering in a document by creating a section, double-click the page icon for the page where you want to create a section.

2 Choose Numbering & Section Options from the Pages palette menu (▶).

3 Select the "Start Page Numbering at" checkbox and enter the page number you want to begin the section. OK the dialog box.

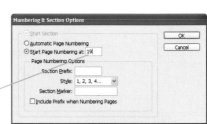

In a facing-pages document, if you section an even-numbered page, but enter an odd number, provided that Allow Pages to Shuffle is selected in the Pages palette menu, the left-hand page becomes a right-hand page and subsequent pages and their contents shuffle: right-hand pages become left-hand pages (and vice versa).

4 The page number indicator below the page icon changes to the number you specify. All subsequent page numbers after the sectioned page are numbered sequentially. The section is identified by a triangle above the section page icon.

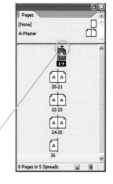

Overriding Master Page Objects

By default, master page objects cannot be edited or manipulated on document pages. You can override master page objects if you want to make changes to them on individual document pages. For example, you might need to amend a strapline set up on a master to indicate a particular section of a publication.

After you create an override on a master page object, you can modify its attributes, such as fill and stroke, position and size, as well as its contents – image or text. When you modify a particular attribute, the attribute you modify is no longer associated with that original attribute on the master. The attribute no longer updates if you change the original attribute on the master page object. Attributes you do not modify remain associated with their equivalent attribute on the master object and update if you make a change to them on the master object.

1 To override a master page object on a document page, working with the Selection tool, hold down Ctrl/Command+Shift and click on the object. It is no longer a protected master page object and can be edited and manipulated as any other object on the page. InDesign refers to this process as creating a "local override".

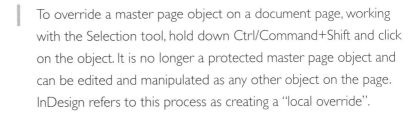

2 To create overrides on all master page objects on a page/spread, double-click on the page number(s) in the Pages palette to target the page/spread, and then choose Override All Master Page Items from the Pages palette menu.

3 To remove an override from a specific object only, select the object, and then choose Remove Selected Local Overrides from the palette menu.

You can detach a master page object from its master page, so that it is completely disassociated from the original master object. To detach a master page object, first create an override for the object, and then choose Detach Selection From Master from the Pages palette menu.

4 If you want to remove all local overrides, double-click on the page number(s) in the Pages palette to target the page/spread; then choose Remove All Local Overrides from the palette menu. This removes local overrides from all objects on the page or spread.

5 To hide all master objects on a page/spread, target the page/spread and choose View>Hide Master Items. Choose View>Show Master Items to make them visible again.

Applying Master Pages

Use the Pages palette to reapply master pages to document pages if you have released master page elements and manipulated them, but now want to return to the standard master page layout. You can also apply a new master page to pages that are currently based on a different master page; for example, you can convert a page based on the A-master to be based on the B-master.

1 To apply either the same master page or a different master, choose Apply Master to Pages from the Pages palette menu (). Specify the master you want to apply from the Apply Master pop-up. Enter the page or page range to which you want to apply the master. Click OK.

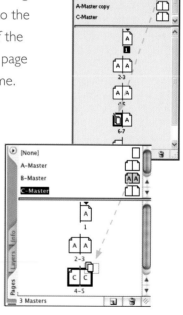

2 To apply a master to a single page, drag the required master page icon onto the page icon in the document area of the Pages palette. Release it when the page icon is highlighted with a black frame.

3 To apply a master to a spread, drag the master page icon to the corner of a spread in the document area. Release it when the spread is highlighted with a black frame.

4 To remove master page objects from a document page, apply the [None] master. [None] is a default master, created when you create a new document.

When you reapply master pages to document pages, master page objects are positioned below page objects in the stacking order. So, for example, if you recolor what was originally a master page color frame on a document page and then reapply the master page, you will not see the reapplied master page element until you move or delete the edited version of it on the document page.

Paragraph, Character & Object Styles

A paragraph style is a collection of paragraph and character settings that control the appearance of complete paragraphs. The settings are saved and appear in the Paragraph Styles palette. Once saved, the paragraph style can be applied to any paragraph in the document quickly and easily, removing the need to recreate the same settings time and time again.

Character styles follow the same basic principles as paragraph styles, but control character settings only. Character styles are used on single characters, words, phrases or sentences; in other words, at a sub-paragraph level.

Object styles help you to apply formatting to objects quickly and consistently throughout a document.

Covers

Chapter Eleven

Paragraph Styles

A paragraph style is a collection of character and paragraph attributes that can be given a name (e.g. Body1) and saved. Once saved, the paragraph style can be quickly and easily applied to individual paragraphs, or ranges of paragraphs, guaranteeing consistency of formatting and also speeding the process of styling text. Paragraph styles control the character and paragraph settings for complete paragraphs.

Style sheets help guarantee consistency within a single document, through a series of related documents (for example, the chapters in a book) and through a series of publications (such as different books in the same series).

As a general rule of thumb, paragraph and character styles are worth creating if you intend to use the same settings more than a couple of times in the same document, or if you want to keep settings consistent across more than one publication.

One of the most significant advantages of using paragraph styles is that if you edit the style description, all paragraphs to which the style has been applied update automatically.

1 To create a paragraph style, choose Type>Paragraph Styles (F11) to show the Paragraph Styles palette, or click the Paragraph Styles tab if the palette is docked in the Palette bar.

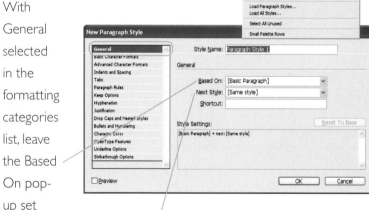

2 Choose New Paragraph Style from the Paragraph Styles palette menu ( ). Enter a name for the paragraph style. With General selected in the formatting categories list, leave the Based On pop-up set to [Basic Paragraph] and Next Style pop-up as [Same style]. To enter a Shortcut, make sure Num Lock is on. Hold down any combination of Ctrl/Command, Alt/option, and Shift, and press any key on the numeric keypad. Setting a shortcut for the style allows you to apply the style without using the mouse when you are styling your text.

When you import a Word file, any Word styles are also imported. A disk icon appears in the Paragraph Styles palette to indicate a style imported from Word. To prevent InDesign from importing Word styles, when you place the Word file, select the Show Import Options checkbox in the Place dialog box. When you click Open, in the Microsoft Word import options dialog box, select the Remove Text and Table Formatting checkbox.

3 Click on formatting category options in the scroll box to choose the categories for which you want to define settings. Settings available in the various categories are covered in detail in individual chapters dealing with character and paragraph formatting, tabs and rules. The most important choices initially are Basic Character Formats (to set attributes such as Font, Size and Leading) and Indents and Spacing (to set alignment options, indents, and the space before and after paragraphs).

4 When you are satisfied with your settings, click OK. The style is listed alphabetically in the Paragraph Styles palette. If you enter a shortcut, this appears to the right of the style name.

5 A useful alternative technique for creating a paragraph style is to base the style on existing formatting already applied to a paragraph. Start by creating the character and paragraph formatting on a paragraph that defines the way you want your text to appear (see Chapters 4 and 5 for information on styling text). Make sure the Text insertion point remains located in the paragraph; then choose New Paragraph Style from the palette menu. The New Paragraph Styles dialog box picks up the settings from the selected text – these are listed in the Style Settings box. If necessary, click on the formatting categories on the left of the dialog box and create or adjust settings as required.

When you create a paragraph style using the technique in Step 5, the paragraph style you create is not automatically applied to the paragraph on which it is based. Make sure you apply the new paragraph style to the original paragraph, if you want this paragraph to update (along with all other paragraphs to which the style is applied) if you make changes to the paragraph style definition at a later stage.

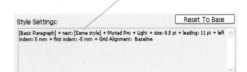

Character Styles

Character styles are used at a sub-paragraph level and control only the character attributes of type – they do not affect paragraph-level attributes such as alignment and indents. Character styles are used to control the appearance of anything from a single character to a word, phrase, sentence, or group of sentences.

As with Paragraph styles, character styles enable you to style text consistently and efficiently throughout a document and across publications.

Use the technique detailed in Step 5 on the previous page to create a character style based on existing formatting. Alternatively, select some text and then press Ctrl/Command+Alt/ option+Shift+C to create a character style definition based on the selected text.

1   To create a character style, choose Type>Character Styles (Shift+F11) to show the Character Styles palette, or click the Character Styles tab if the palette is docked in the Palette bar. There are no existing character styles to choose from in the default Character Styles palette.

2   Choose New Character Style from the Character Styles palette menu (▶).

3   Enter a name for the style in the Style Name entry field.

You can only use numbers on the number keypad as shortcuts for paragraph and character styles – you cannot use letters or non-keypad numbers.

4   Make sure Based On is set to [None] to simplify working with styles when you first start to use them.

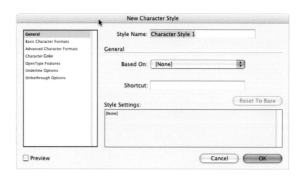

5 Enter a shortcut for the character style in the Shortcut field if desired. Shortcuts allow you to apply character styles using the keyboard instead of the mouse, and can be very useful. Make sure Num Lock is on to set a shortcut; then hold down any combination of Ctrl/Command, Alt/option and Shift, and type a number on the numeric keypad.

6 Click on style options in the scroll box on the left to select formatting categories for which you want to define settings. (Individual options available are covered in Chapter 4).

7 Choose Character Color from the scroll box if you want to specify a different Fill and/or Stroke color for the text. Make sure you select either the Fill or Stroke icon (as appropriate) before you click on a color swatch.

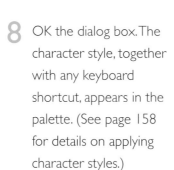

8 OK the dialog box. The character style, together with any keyboard shortcut, appears in the palette. (See page 158 for details on applying character styles.)

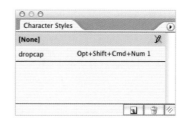

Applying Styles

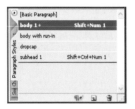

Before you apply paragraph or character styles, make sure you highlight an appropriate range of text.

1. To apply a paragraph style, select the Type tool; click into a paragraph to apply the style to one paragraph only, or highlight a range of paragraphs.

2. Click on the paragraph style name in the Paragraph Styles palette to apply it. Alternatively, make sure that Num Lock is on, and enter the shortcut you specified when you set up the style. Character styles and any local formatting overrides are retained when you apply a paragraph style.

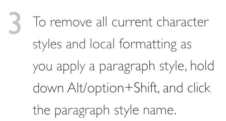

3. To remove all current character styles and local formatting as you apply a paragraph style, hold down Alt/option+Shift, and click the paragraph style name.

4. To preserve all character styles in the text, but remove local formatting overrides as you apply a paragraph style, hold down Alt/option, and click on the paragraph style name.

5 For a paragraph with styles applied to it, you can click [Basic Paragraph] to disassociate the paragraph from the styles. Clicking [Basic Paragraph] does not change the appearance of the paragraph (as the formatting

remains intact), but any changes you make to the original paragraph or character style settings will not be reflected in the paragraph subsequently.

You can also clear formatting overrides by clicking the Clear Formatting Overrides button in the bottom of the Paragraph Styles palette:

6 To apply a character style, highlight a range of characters – from a single character upwards. Click on a character style in the Character Styles palette. You can also use the shortcut if you set one up, but make sure that Num Lock is on before you use a keyboard shortcut to apply a style. Character styles change only the settings that are specified in the style.

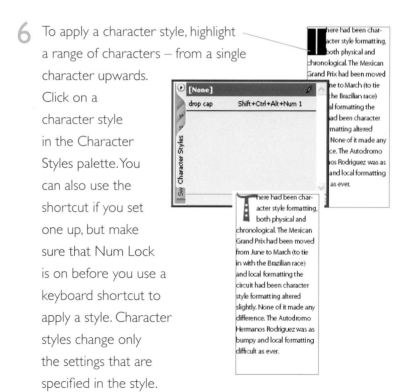

Editing Styles

Select the Preview option in the Style Options dialog box to see a preview of the result of changes you make to settings before you OK the dialog box.

The basic principles and techniques for editing paragraph and character styles are the same. When you edit a style, text to which the style has been applied is updated automatically to reflect the new settings. This is a powerful reason for working with paragraph and character styles.

1 To edit a style, click on the style you want to edit in either the Paragraph or Character Styles palette. Choose Style Options from the Paragraph or Character Styles palette menu ().

Click the Reset to Base button to quickly reset a child style to match the parent style on which it is based.

2 Use the Style Options dialog box to modify any settings you want to change. The options are identical to those available

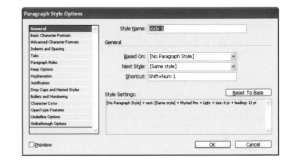

when you first set up the style. Click OK. The change is applied throughout the document wherever the style is already applied.

3 Use the Redefine Style command to redefine a style based on selected text. First, select some text currently formatted with the style you want to redefine. Change the Character and Paragraph settings as required. Then choose Redefine Style from the palette menu, or use the shortcut: Ctrl/Command+Alt/option+Shift+R.

If you delete a style that is in use in the document, the Delete Paragraph Style prompt appears. Use the Delete Style and Replace With pop-up menu to replace the deleted style, wherever it is used in the document, with another available style.

4 To delete a style, click on the style name to select it; then choose Delete Style from the palette menu, or click the Wastebasket icon at the bottom of the palette. Alternatively, you can drag the style name onto the Wastebasket.

Copying Styles

To save the work of recreating a complex set of both paragraph and character styles when you need to establish a consistent identity across a range of publications, you can load or copy individual styles or complete sets of styles from one document to another.

1 To load styles into a document, first make sure the Paragraph or Character Styles palette is showing. From the palette menu, choose Load Paragraph/ Character Styles, depending on which palette is active.

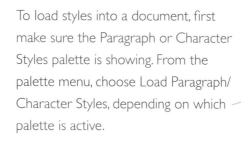

2 In the Open File dialog box, use standard Windows/ Mac techniques to navigate to the document with the

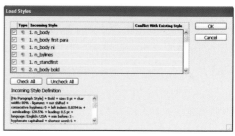

styles you want to copy. Click on the name of the file; then click the Open button. Use the checkboxes on the left of the Load Styles dialog box to specify the styles you want to import. You can click the Check All or Uncheck All button to quickly select or deselect all available styles. Click OK when you finish making your selection, to copy the styles into your InDesign document.

3 An alternative technique is to highlight some styled text in a different document. Choose Edit>Copy to copy the text to the clipboard. Move to the document into which you want to copy the styles. Create a text frame; then paste the text into the frame. The text is pasted into the document and any paragraph or character styles are appended to the document's Paragraph and Character Styles palettes. This is a useful technique for selectively copying styles from one document to another.

Nested Styles

A nested style is a combination of one or more character styles applied at the beginning of a paragraph – for example, to a drop cap or a run-in heading – at the same time as a paragraph style.

1 To create a nested style, begin by creating the character style you want to use at the start of a paragraph.

2 Either double-click the paragraph style you want to contain the nested style, or select the paragraph style and then choose Style Options from the palette menu. Click the Drop Caps and Nested Styles option from the formatting categories scroll box on the left.

3 Click the New Nested Style button to activate the Nested Styles pop-up menus, which allow you to set parameters for the nested style.

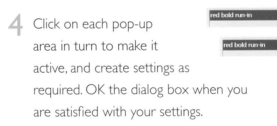

4 Click on each pop-up area in turn to make it active, and create settings as required. OK the dialog box when you are satisfied with your settings.

News in brief

Country clothing manufacturer John Walker plans to expand its retail operation next year with the launch of a new concept shop.

The new company is looking for a site in London, but would also consider opening in mainland Europe if a suitable unit was not found in the UK.

The strategy behind the concept shop is to provide a unit which could be used as a model for further growth into concessions and shop-in shops.

5 Apply the paragraph style to see the result. The nested character style is applied automatically along with the paragraph style.

Object Styles

Create object styles to improve efficiency and reduce the amount of time it takes to create objects with consistent formatting. Formatting attributes you can apply using object styles include fill and stroke, text wrap, text frame options, transparency and drop shadow controls as well as paragraph styles.

Creating an Object Style

1 Create an object and apply the settings such as fill, stroke and text wrap that you want to include in the object style.

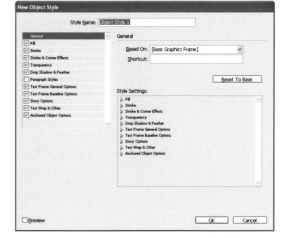

2 Choose Window>Object Styles to show the Object Styles palette if it is not already showing.

3 Select the object using the Selection tool; then choose New Object Style from the Object Styles palette menu.

4 In the New Object Style dialog box, enter a name for the style.

As you begin to work with Object Styles it is probably best to leave all General options checked as they are by default.

5 In the General categories on the left hand side of the dialog box, deselect the checkboxes for features you do not want to include in the object style.

6   Click OK when you are satisfied with the settings in the dialog box. The new object stye appears in the Object Styles palette along with any keyboard shortcut you assigned to it.

Options

Based on – You can base a new object style on an existing object style. The existing object style functions as the parent style; the new style functions as a child style. When you modify a parent style, any attributes it shares with a child style update in the child style according to the change you make. Any settings that the child style does not share are not changed. You can use the Based on feature so that changes you make to a parent style ripple through the related styles that are based on it.

You must be very careful and deliberate about the way in which you use the "Based on" feature. It is probably best to set it to [None] until you have gained experience and control in using object styles.

Shortcut – Hold down a modifier key, such as Shift or Command, or a combination of modifier keys; then type a number on the number keypad to create a shortcut for the Object Style.

Style Settings – In the Style Settings area of the New Object Style dialog box, you can use the style categories to establish exactly what formatting attributes and values are applied to the selected object. Click the Expand/Collapse triangle to reveal details for each category.

Click the Reset to Base button to quickly reset a child style to match the parent style on which it is based.

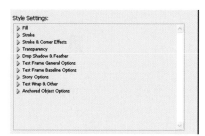

Style Settings:
- Fill
- Stroke
- Stroke & Corner Effects
- Transparency
- Drop Shadow & Feather
- Text Frame General Options
- Text Frame Baseline Options
- Story Options
- Text Wrap & Other
- Anchored Object Options

Applying Object Styles

1   To apply an object style, select an object you want to style.

2   Click on the object style name in the Object Styles palette, or use the keyboard shortcut you set in the New Object Style dialog box. You can also choose an object style from the Style pop-up menu in the Control palette.

red dotted arrow

Tables and Tabs

Whenever you need to organize data into regular rows and columns, the table functionality built into InDesign offers a wide variety of flexible and creative options. Working with InDesign tables, you can control the appearance of cells, rows, columns, grid lines and borders, as well as specifying exact widths and heights for cells.

Use tabs when you want to align columns of figures or text accurately in tabular information such as timetables and price lists.

Covers

Inserting a Table

Typically, a table consists of a group of cells, arranged in a grid-like structure, that hold related data, which can consist of text and/or images. In many instances, you have greater control using a table than using tabs to create the regular horizontal and vertical spacing of information across and down the page, especially when the graphic appearance of the table is an important consideration.

1 Use the Type tool to draw a text frame that is roughly the size of the table you want to create. You do not have to be exact at this stage, as you can make the frame fit the final size of the table later.

2 With the Text insertion point located in the frame, choose Table>Insert Table. In the Insert Table dialog box, enter the number of columns and rows you want in the table. Enter values for Header Rows and Footer Rows if your table will span across columns or pages and you want certain rows to repeat at the top (Header Rows) and/or bottom (Footer Rows) of each column/page the table covers.

You can insert a table at the Text insertion point in the middle of running copy. The table then handles like an inline graphic. You can use the Space Before/Space After fields in the Table Setup dialog box (Table>Table Options>Table Setup) to control the amount of space above and below the table.

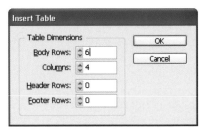

3 Click OK. The table structure appears in the text frame. InDesign creates a table with default size cells that fill the width of the text frame. The height of the cells is initially determined by the slug height of the type, which is relative to the default type size that is currently set. The table has 1-point vertical and horizontal grid lines applied by default.

In the context of table cell height, the "slug" height refers to the size of the black highlight area of selected text:

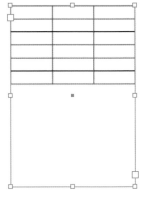

Adding and Deleting Rows/Columns

Unless you know the exact contents of a table at the outset, you will probably need to add or delete rows and/or columns to achieve the final table structure you require.

1 To change the number of rows/columns in a table, make sure you are working with the Type tool. Click into the table to place the Text insertion point in a cell.

2 Choose Table>Table Options>Table Setup (Ctrl/Command+Alt/ option+Shift+B). Enter

new values for Body Rows and Columns as required. OK the dialog box. If you reduce the number of rows or columns, a warning prompt appears. Click OK if you want to proceed.

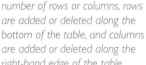

When you use the Table Options dialog box, or the Table palette, to change the number of rows or columns, rows are added or deleted along the bottom of the table, and columns are added or deleted along the right-hand edge of the table.

3 Alternatively, use the Table palette to change the number of rows/columns. Choose Window>Type & Tables>Table (Shift+F9) to show the Table palette if it is not already showing. Change the values in the Number of Rows/ Columns fields as required.

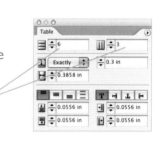

4 For more precision when adding rows or columns, position your cursor in a cell, and then choose Table>Insert>Column or Row. Enter the number of columns or rows

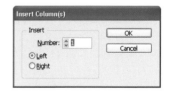

you want to create, and specify whether you want the columns inserted to the right or left of the column where the cursor is located, or rows above or below where the cursor is located.

Moving from Cell to Cell

To work efficiently and productively in tables, especially tables with a lot of detail and precise formatting requirements, you need to be able to move quickly and accurately around the cells in the table structure.

If you press the Tab key when the Text insertion point is located in the last cell of the table, you create an additional row in the table.

1. Working with the Type tool, click in any cell to position the Text insertion point in that cell.

2. To move the Text insertion point from cell to cell, you can press the Up/Down/Left/Right arrow keys. You can also press the Tab key to move the cursor cell by cell to the right. When the insertion point reaches the end of a row it then continues in the first cell of the next row down.

Get into the habit of choosing the Type tool when you work with tables. Most actions you perform on a table use this tool.

3. To move the Text insertion point backward through the table, hold down Shift and press the Tab key.

4. Hold down Alt/option and press Page Up/PageDown to move the cursor to the first/last cell in the column.

5. Hold down Alt/option and press Home/End to move the cursor to the first/last cell in a row.

6. In large tables with many rows it can be useful to jump quickly to a specific row. Choose Table>Go to Row. Enter the row number and then click OK. Use the Row pop-up menu to choose Header or Footer rows if required.

Highlighting Techniques

To control the formatting and appearance of a table you must be able to highlight its various parts to suit the task in hand. The most essential tool for working with tables is the Type tool.

1 To select the entire table, working with the Type tool, position your cursor on the top left corner of the table.

Schnobler	1 Year Bond maturity date 08/10/06	2 Year Bond maturity date 08/10/07	3 Year Bond maturity date 08/10/08	10 Year Bond maturity date 08/10/16
Issue No.	ZX	ZY	ZZ	ZZZ
Year 1	7.35%	7.55%	7.85%	7.95%
Year 2	7.95%	8.35%	8.35%	8.65%
Year 3	9.95%	9.35%	9.35%	9.65%
Year 4	9.95%	9.95%	9.95%	9.95%

The cursor changes to the Table select cursor (⬕). Click once to select the entire table. This is useful when you want to work globally on the table, for example to set type size and font for every cell in the table. Alternatively, choose Table>Select>Table (Ctrl/Command+Alt/option+A).

2 To select an entire row, position your cursor on the left edge of the row you want to select. The cursor changes to the Row select cursor

Schnobler	1 Year Bond maturity date 08/10/06	2 Year Bond maturity date 08/10/07	3 Year Bond maturity date 08/10/08	10 Year Bond maturity date 08/10/16
Issue No.	ZX	ZY	ZZ	ZZZ
Year 1	7.35%	7.55%	7.85%	7.95%
Year 2	7.95%	8.35%	8.35%	8.65%
Year 3	9.95%	9.35%	9.35%	9.65%
Year 4	9.95%	9.95%	9.95%	9.95%

(➔). Click to select the row. Alternatively, with the Text insertion point in a cell, choose Table>Select>Row (Ctrl/Command+3).

3 To select an entire column, position your cursor on the top edge of the column you want to select. The cursor changes

Schnobler	1 Year Bond maturity date 08/10/06	2 Year Bond maturity date 08/10/07	3 Year Bond maturity date 08/10/08	10 Year Bond maturity date 08/10/16
Issue No.	ZX	ZY	ZZ	ZZZ
Year 1	7.35%	7.55%	7.85%	7.95%
Year 2	7.95%	8.35%	8.35%	8.65%
Year 3	9.95%	9.35%	9.35%	9.65%
Year 4	9.95%	9.95%	9.95%	9.95%

to the Column select cursor (⬇). Click once to select the column. Alternatively, with the Text insertion point in a cell, choose Table>Select>Column (Ctrl/Command+Alt/option+3).

Resizing Columns and Rows

As you create a table, you will need to control the width of columns and the height of cells to create the table structure you require. You can resize columns and rows manually with the mouse, or you can enter exact values to achieve the results you want. Remember to work with the Type tool when you want to make changes to the structural appearance of a table.

The slug height, which is relative to the type size set for a row, determines the minimum height for cells in the row, even if there is no actual type in any of the cells. When you drag a cell border to resize a row's height, you cannot make it shorter than the height needed to accommodate the slug. Reduce the type size set for a row if you need to reduce the row height further.

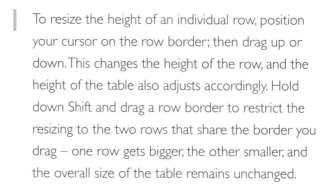

1 To resize the height of an individual row, position your cursor on the row border; then drag up or down. This changes the height of the row, and the height of the table also adjusts accordingly. Hold down Shift and drag a row border to restrict the resizing to the two rows that share the border you drag – one row gets bigger, the other smaller, and the overall size of the table remains unchanged.

2 To resize all rows in the table proportionally, position your cursor on the bottom edge of a table, hold down Shift, and drag.

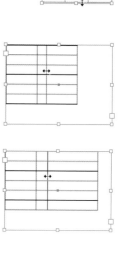

3 To resize the width of an individual column, position your cursor on the column border, and drag left or right. This changes the width of the column, and the width of the table also adjusts accordingly. Hold down Shift and drag a column border to restrict the resizing to the two columns that share the border you drag – one column gets wider, the other narrower, and the overall width of the table remains unchanged.

As you make changes to the width and height of columns and rows in a table, the table itself may extend beyond the boundaries of the text frame in which it is located:

In such an instance you can either use the Selection tool to change the width of the text frame manually, or choose Object>Fitting>Fit Frame to Content (Ctrl/Command+Alt/option+C) to match the size of the frame to the size of the table it contains.

Choose Window>Type & Tables>Table (Shift+F9) to show the Table palette if it is not already showing. Remember to rest your cursor on the icons in the Table palette to reveal the tool tips, which will help you to identify the control you want to use:

4 To resize all columns proportionally, position your cursor on the right edge of a table, hold down Shift, and then drag.

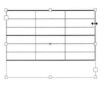

Resizing Columns and Rows Precisely

1 To resize a row to an exact height, select the row using the Row selection cursor (➡). (Drag with the Row selection cursor to select more than one consecutive row.) Choose Table>Cell Options>Rows and Columns. With the Rows and Columns tab selected, select Exactly from the Row Height pop-up; then enter the row height you require in the entry field.

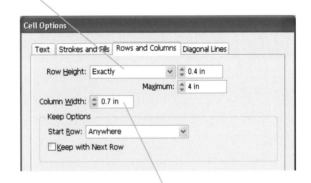

2 To resize a column to an exact width, select the column using the Column selection cursor (⬇). (Drag with the Column selection cursor to select more than one consecutive column.) Choose Table>Cell Options>Rows and Columns. With the Rows and Columns tab selected, enter the width you require in the Column Width entry field.

3 As an alternative to using the Cell Options dialog box, you can use the Table palette to specify exact width and height settings for selected rows or columns.

Entering Content in Cells

When you have a suitable table structure you can start to enter text and images into individual cells.

Entering Text

1. Select the Type tool; then click into a cell to place the Text insertion point. Begin typing. Text will wrap when it reaches the edge of the cell. Provided that you have not specified an exact height for the row, the cell will expand downward as you enter more and more text.

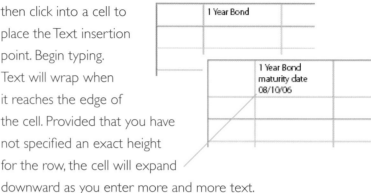

If you have specified an exact height for a row and you enter more text than will fit into the cell, the excess text becomes overmatter. You cannot thread overset text into another cell.

2. If you have set an exact height for the row and you enter more text than will fit, the additional text becomes overset text and the overset cell marker appears.

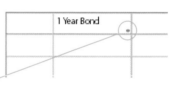

You can also paste text from the clipboard into a cell, or use File>Place to import text into a cell.

3. To highlight overset text in a cell (for example, so that you can reduce the type size so that it fits into the cell), click to place the Text insertion point in the cell, and then choose Edit>Select All (Ctrl/Command+A).

Placing an Image in a Cell

1. To place an image into a table cell, it is best if you make sure that the image will fit into the cell before you place it. Working with the Type tool, click into the cell to place the Text insertion point. Choose

	1 Year Bond maturity date 08/10/06	2 Year Bon maturity d
Issue No.	ZX	ZY
Year 1	7.35%	7.55%

File>Place, and then use standard Windows/Mac techniques to locate the file. Select the file, and click the Open button to place the image into the cell.

2 Provided that you have not specified an exact height for the cells in the row, a cell expands downward if an image is deeper than the initial depth of the cell. If you add an image to a cell with a fixed height and the image is taller than the cell height, the cell is overset and the overset cell marker appears. To correct this you must make either the image smaller or the cell larger. An image that is wider than the cell you place it in extends beyond the right-hand edge of the cell.

Schnoble	1 Year Bond maturity date 08/10/06	2 Year Bon maturity d
Issue No.	ZX	ZY
Year 1	7.35%	7.55%

3 For an image that extends beyond the right-hand edge of a cell, select the content of the cell by pressing the Esc key, and then choose Table>Cell Options>Text. Select the Clip Contents to Cell checkbox to hide any part of the image that extends beyond the right-hand edge of the cell.

Clipping
☑ Clip Contents to Cell

Schnob	1 Year Bond maturity date 08/10/06	2 Year Bond maturity dat
Issue No.	ZX	ZY
Year 1	7.35%	7.55%

Cell Controls

Use the Text tab of the Cell Options dialog box to control how text sits within a cell. The range of available options is similar to those found in the Text Frame Options dialog box.

1 Working with the Type tool, make sure you have the Text insertion point located in a cell, or select columns, rows or the entire table, depending on the range of cells you want to change. Choose Table>Cell Options>Text.

2 To create additional space on the inside of a cell, enter Cell Inset values for Top/ Bottom/Left/Right as required.

3 To align content vertically in a cell (for example, if you want to center text in a cell vertically), select an option from the Vertical Justification Align pop-up menu.

4 To rotate text in a cell, choose a rotation amount from the Rotation pop-up menu. The overset cell marker ( ) appears if the rotated text does not fit within the dimensions of the cell.

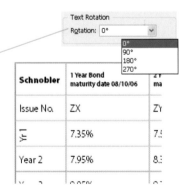

Cell Strokes, Borders and Fills

When you create a table it appears with a default 1-point, black border and 1-point, black vertical and horizontal grid lines. You can hide or show the border and grid lines, and there is a wide variety of customization options.

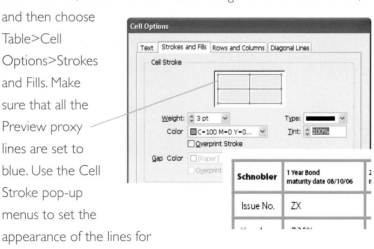

1 To make changes to the border, select the Type tool, and then click into a cell in the table. Choose Table>Table Options>Table Setup. Use the Table Border pop-up menus to control the appearance of the border. To remove the border, either set the Weight to zero, or select None from the Type pop-up menu. Click OK to apply the settings.

Make sure you select a line Type when you create settings for a border. If you set a Weight, but the Type is set to None, the border does not appear.

2 To make changes to all vertical and horizontal grid lines as well as the border, select the entire table using the Table select cursor, and then choose Table>Cell Options>Strokes and Fills. Make sure that all the Preview proxy lines are set to blue. Use the Cell Stroke pop-up menus to set the appearance of the lines for the table. Click OK.

In the Strokes and Fills tab of the Cell Options dialog box, click the proxy lines to toggle them from blue (selected) to gray (not selected). Changes to settings are applied to cell borders represented by the blue lines, and do not affect cell borders represented by the gray lines:

3 To make changes to an individual cell or a series of selected cells, either click into a single cell or highlight a range of cells. Choose Table>Cell Options> Strokes and Fills. In the Cell Stroke tab of the Cell Options dialog box, click the proxy lines to toggle them from blue (selected) to gray (not selected) so that the settings you create are only applied to the selected borders for the selected cells.

Schnobler	1 Year Bond maturity date 08/10/06	2' m
Issue No.	ZX	

Cell Fill

As well as controlling stroke attributes for cell borders in a table, you can specify the fill color for individual cells, a range of highlighted cells or the entire table.

1 Make sure you are working with the Type tool, and select the range of cells you want to change.

2 Choose Table>Cell Options>Strokes and Fills. In the Cell Fill area of the dialog box, use the Color pop-up menu to select a color from the existing range of color swatches available in the Swatches palette. Use the Tint entry box to specify a tint from 0–100%. OK the dialog box to apply the setting.

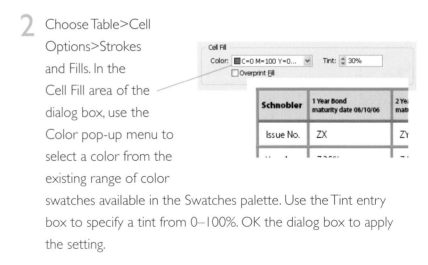

Alternating Fills and Strokes

InDesign tables provide a range of versatile controls for setting up alternating fill patterns for rows and columns, and also alternating stroke controls for vertical and horizontal grid lines in a table. Using alternating fill and/or stroke controls, especially in a complex table with a considerable number of rows, can help make the data it contains more readable and more easily understood.

Alternating Fills

Alternating Fill controls apply to an entire table. Select the Preserve Local Formatting option in the Table Options dialog box if you want to retain formatting already applied to specific cells, rows or columns.

1 To set up alternating fills for a table, working with the Type tool, click in a cell to position the Text insertion point. Choose Table>Table Options>Alternating Fills.

2 Select an option from the Alternating Pattern pop-up to specify the frequency with which the pattern repeats. You can also set up custom patterns by entering values in the First and Next entry boxes: enter values that are different in First and Next to set up an irregular repeating pattern.

You can specify alternating patterns for rows or columns in a table, but not both. Use the same principles for alternating columns as demonstrated on this page for alternating rows.

3 Use the Color pop-ups to select colors from the existing range of colors in the Swatches palette. Specify a tint using the Tint entry fields.

4 Enter values for Skip First/Skip Last for rows at the top or bottom of the table that you do not want included in the repeating pattern because you want to format them individually.

5 If you have formatted some cells individually, you can retain the individual formatting characteristics when using alternating fill controls by selecting the Preserve local formatting option in the Fills tab of the Table Options dialog box.

Alternating Strokes

Setting up alternating stroke patterns on the vertical and/or horizontal grid lines of a table is similar to setting up alternating fill patterns. You can combine alternating fills and alternating strokes.

The Column Strokes tab of the Table Options dialog box provides exactly the same set of options as the Row Strokes tab.

1 To set up alternating strokes for a table, working with the Type tool, click in any cell to position the Text insertion point. Choose Table>Table Options>Alternating Row Strokes.

2 Select an option from the Alternating Pattern pop-up to specify the frequency with which the alternating stroke pattern repeats. You can also set up custom patterns by entering values in the First and Next entry boxes: enter values that are different in First and Next to set up an irregular repeating pattern.

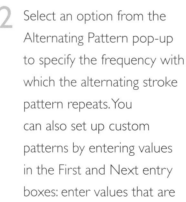

3 Use the Color pop-ups to select stroke colors from the swatches available in the Swatches palette. Specify a tint using the Tint entry fields.

4 Enter values for Skip First/Skip Last for rows at the top or bottom of the table that you do not want included in the repeating pattern.

Importing Tables

When you import a Microsoft Excel spreadsheet, or a Word document that contains a table, the imported data is automatically formatted as an InDesign table. If you cut and paste data from Excel, or a Word table, it appears as tabbed text in InDesign.

Importing from Excel

1. To import an Excel spreadsheet, first use the Type tool to create a text frame. With the Text insertion point located in the text frame, choose File>Place. Use standard Windows/Mac techniques to navigate to the file you want to import. Click on the file to select it; then click the Open button.

If you have imported tabbed text from another application, you can convert it into a table. Select the tabbed text using the Type tool; then choose Table>Convert Text to Table to convert the text into an InDesign table with default formatting.

2. In the Options area, create settings that are specific to the properties of your Excel spreadsheet.

3. In the Formatting section, use the Table pop-up menu to specify how the table appears initially in InDesign. Select Formatted Table if you want InDesign to attempt to preserve and import as much of the native Excel table formatting as possible. Select Unformatted Table if you want InDesign to apply its default table formatting to the imported data. Select Unformatted Tabbed Text to import the data as tabbed text – not into an InDesign table. Click OK.

4. The spreadsheet data appears in an InDesign table according to the options you set in the Microsoft Excel Import Options dialog box.

As an alternative to creating a text frame before you choose the Place command, you can choose Place, select and open a Word or Excel file, and then use the Loaded text cursor to manually define the width and height of the text frame into which you want to import the data.

Importing Word Tables

InDesign can import Word tables as InDesign tables, which you can manipulate and format as required.

1. To import a Word table, use the Type tool to create a text frame. Make sure the Text insertion point is located in the frame; then choose File>Place. Use standard Windows/Mac techniques to locate the file you want to import. Click on the file to select it.

2. In the Place dialog box, you can select Show Import Options if you want to make changes to the way in which InDesign imports the table data. Then click the Open button.

If you copy and paste Excel data or a Word table into InDesign, it appears as tabbed text. Select the tabbed text, and then choose Table>Convert Text to Table to convert the text into an InDesign table with default formatting.

3. If you selected Show Import Options, select the Remove Styles and Formatting from Text and Tables option to remove formatting such as typeface and type style from any imported text as well as Word tables. Selecting this option

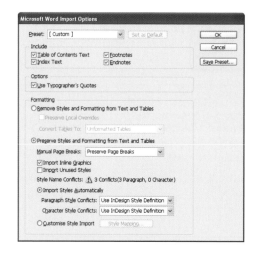

also prevents paragraph styles from being imported with the text. Leave the option unselected if you want InDesign to attempt to preserve as much of the original Word formatting as possible.

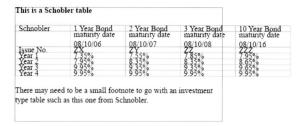

Setting and Editing Tabs

When you begin working with tabs it is often easiest to set the tabs when the text frame is empty, and then enter your text and adjust the tabs as necessary to get the table to work.

Use tabs to line up columns of figures and text accurately. There is a temptation to use spaces for aligning entries in tabular information, but this can be inaccurate and unnecessarily time-consuming. With practice you will come to appreciate the accuracy and versatility of tabs for producing professional results.

Tabs are a paragraph attribute. If your Text insertion point is flashing in a paragraph when you enter the Tabs palette, you set tabs for that specific paragraph. Remember to highlight a range of paragraphs to set or edit tabs for more than one paragraph.

You can use the keyboard shortcut Ctrl/Command+ Shift+T to show the Tabs palette.

1 To set tabs for an empty text frame, click into it with the Type tool, to place the Text insertion point. Choose Type>Tabs. The Tabs palette appears along the top of the selected frame. Provided the top of the frame is visible, the palette snaps to the top of the frame and matches the width of the first column. Initially, the left edge of the frame and the zero point of the Tabs palette ruler line up. This is useful as a visual reference for setting tabs. If you reposition the Tabs palette and then want to realign it to the text frame, or if you want to snap the Tabs palette to the same width as the text frame, click the Magnet button to the right of the palette.

The gray ticks, set at regular intervals, that appear initially on the Tab ruler represent the default tab stops:

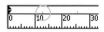

As you set your own tab stops, default tabs to the left of the tab you set disappear automatically.

2 Choose a tab alignment type by clicking on one of the tab alignment buttons: Left, Center, Right or Decimal.

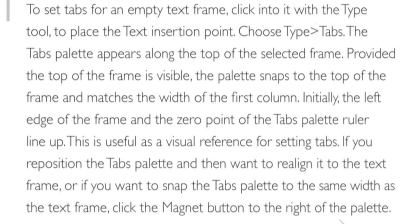

3 Click on the tab ruler to position a tab manually. The tab is indicated by a tab marker on the ruler. Initially the tab is selected, indicated by a blue highlight on the tab. Drag the tab to fine-tune its position. Alternatively, enter a value in the X entry field to specify the position for the selected tab. Press Enter/Return to set the tab marker on the ruler.

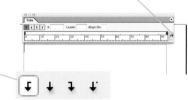

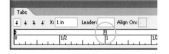

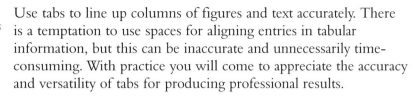

If necessary, you can manually reposition the Tab palette so that the zero point of the ruler lines up with the left edge of the text frame, and then use the resize icon of the palette to match the width of the ruler to the width of the text frame.

4 Repeat Steps 2–3 until you have set as many tabs as you need. Either close the palette, or leave it showing until you have finished fine-tuning the table.

5 If you want to set tabs at equal distances across the text frame, set the first tab marker, and then choose Repeat Tab from the Tab palette menu (▶). Tabs are repeated based on the distance from the left margin of the text frame to the initial tab marker.

6 Enter the text for the table in the text frame. Press the Tab key each time you need to line up text or numbers at a particular tab stop position.

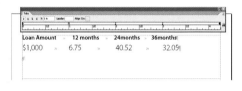

Deleting Tabs

You can delete individual tabs or you can delete all tabs for a paragraph or a range of paragraphs. Deleting all tabs can be useful when you receive text that has been set up with tabs in a wordprocessing application. Typically such tabs are not going to work in a page layout with different margin and column settings.

To delete a tab, select the Type tool; then click into a paragraph in a text frame, or highlight a range of paragraphs. Choose Type>Tabs. If you highlight a range of paragraphs containing different tab settings, the tab markers for the first highlighted paragraph appear as normal; tab markers for the other highlighted paragraphs with different tab stops appear gray. It is best to avoid deleting tabs when you have mixed tab settings. Reselect paragraphs more accurately to avoid getting mixed settings.

...cont'd

If your Text insertion point is flashing in a text frame, and you make changes to tab markers in the Tabs palette, these changes affect only the tabs in the paragraph where the Text insertion point is flashing, not the entire text frame.

When you are working with tabular information it can be useful to show hidden characters (Type>Show Hidden Characters or Ctrl/Command+Alt/option+I), so that you can see exactly where and how many tab stops you have inserted in the text. Tab stop hidden characters are represented by a blue chevron:

To change the alignment for a tab, click on the tab marker in the ruler to select it, and then click on a different tab-alignment button:

2 Position your cursor on the tab marker you want to delete, and then drag it off the Tab palette ruler. Do not press the Backspace or Delete keys – these will delete highlighted text and not tab markers. To delete all tabs, choose Clear All from the Tabs palette menu.

Clear All
Repeat Tab

Editing Tabs

Getting a tabbed table to work can sometimes be a tricky business. You often end up having to edit tabs and fine-tune text to get a professional, finished result. When editing tabs, take care to select the specific range of paragraphs whose tabs you want to change.

1 To edit tabs, highlight a range of paragraphs, and then choose Type>Tabs. Click once on a tab marker to highlight it. Its numeric position appears in the X entry field. Enter a new value, and then press Enter/Return to apply the change. The tab marker moves to its new position and text in the highlighted paragraphs moves according to the new tab setting.

2 You can manually adjust a tab marker by dragging it along the tab ruler. As you do so, a vertical line appears to indicate the position of the tab in the table. This can be extremely useful as an aid in positioning

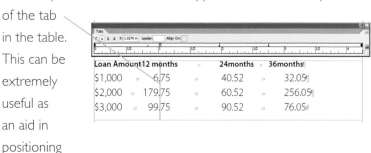

the tab marker exactly where you want it. The X entry field gives a numeric read-out as you drag the tab marker. Text in the highlighted paragraphs realigns when you release the mouse. Repeat the process as necessary; then close the Tabs palette when you are satisfied.

Leader Dots

When you set a tab stop, you have the option of setting leader dots leading up to the tab position. Leader dots help the eye to follow across a row of information in detailed tables, such as railway timetables, which consist of columns of figures that are not easily differentiated. In such a table, it is easy for the eye to wander up or down as it moves across each row. Leader dots help prevent this from happening.

1   To set leader dots for a tab, make sure you have selected an appropriate range of paragraphs with the Type tool. Choose Type>Tabs.

2   In the tab ruler, click on the tab that you want leader dots to run up to. The tab is highlighted and its position appears in the X field.

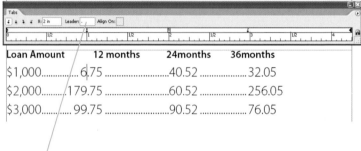

3   Enter up to eight characters in the Leader entry field. Typically you will use a full stop. You can create a less dense leader by entering a combination of full stops and spaces. You do not have to use full stops as leader symbols – you can use any character on your keyboard.

4   To set up a leader as you create your tab stops, enter characters in the Leader field when the tab stop you are setting is highlighted.

Table of Contents, Indexing and Books

The Book palette makes it possible to organize long documents (such as books or technical manuals), consisting of separate but related InDesign documents, which you need to work on as individual documents while maintaining a consistent style throughout. You can also create tables of contents and indexes for an entire publication by organizing documents as a "book".

The Index palette provides the functionality to produce a professional index for an individual document, or for a series of InDesign documents set up as a book.

The Table of Contents functionality brings together, in a single text story, paragraphs (such as headings or titles) that have been styled using paragraph styles. You can create Tables of Contents for individual documents or an entire book.

Covers

Chapter Thirteen

Table of Contents Style Setup

Provided that you have used paragraph styles to format elements, such as titles and headings, consistently throughout a document, you can use the Table of Contents functionality to automate the process of building the table of contents. Essentially, the table of contents brings together, in a single text file, all paragraphs with a particular paragraph style applied to them.

1   A simple table of contents typically consists of a title, the content entries and their page number references. Before you can generate the table of contents you must set up a Table of Contents Style, which indicates to InDesign the paragraph styles it is to include when creating the contents, and also specifies the appearance of the various elements in the table of contents.

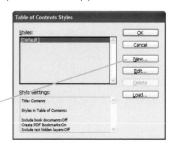

Chapter Contents

2   Choose Layout>Table of Content Styles. Click the New button to go into the New Table of Contents Style dialog box.

If you are defining a table of contents style for a book, make sure you have the Book palette open. You can then choose to associate the TOC Style to the book by selecting the Include Book Document checkbox.

3   Enter a name for the style in the TOC Style field. This serves as a label that you will use to refer to the style you are about to set up.

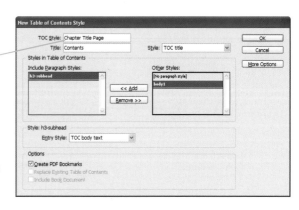

4 Enter a title for the table of contents if you want it to say something other than Contents when you generate it. From the Style pop-up, select a paragraph style to control the appearance of the title. TOC title, which appears in the pop-up, is a default style created by InDesign. It is a good idea to create your own paragraph style before you begin the process of creating a Table of Contents Style, so that it is available in this pop-up. If you choose TOC title, the paragraph style is automatically added to your Paragraph Styles palette when you click OK to complete the new TOC style setup.

Select the Create PDF Bookmarks option in the Options area of the dialog box to automatically add table of contents entries when you export the file as a PDF.

5 In the Styles in Table of Contents area, click on a paragraph style in the Other Styles list, and then click the Add button to move it into the Include Paragraph Styles list. This marks the style so that InDesign can generate a table of contents based on all paragraphs to which the style is applied. You can add more than one paragraph style.

If you use the default TOC styles, they are added to the Paragraph Styles palette when you complete the new style process. You can create a Table of Contents style using the InDesign default paragraph styles, and then edit these to suit your purposes at a later stage.

6 To control the appearance of the contents entries, use the Entry Style pop-up in the Style area to choose a paragraph style. Again, TOC body text, which appears in the list, is a default style created by InDesign. It is a good idea to create your own style for this purpose beforehand. If you have more than one style in the Include Paragraph Styles list, click on each in turn and choose a formatting style from the Entry Style pop-up.

7 Click the OK button when you are satisfied with your settings, to return to the Table of Contents Styles dialog box. OK this dialog box to complete the setup process.

Creating a Table of Contents

When you have applied paragraph styles throughout the document to elements such as titles and subheads that you want to include in a table of contents, and you have created a Table of Contents Style, you can proceed to generate the table of contents.

1 Choose Layout>Table of Contents. If you have set up more than one Table of Contents style, make sure you choose the appropriate style from the TOC Style pop-up menu. The Table of Contents dialog box displays the same settings as the ones you set up when you initially created the TOC style.

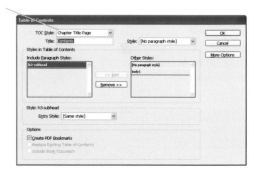

2 At this stage, you can adjust any of the settings to create a custom Table of Contents style based on the settings initially displayed. This does not change the specifications of the Style – just this instance.

3 Click OK to generate the table of contents as a new text file. Use the Loaded text cursor to place the table of contents into an existing text frame, or press and drag the cursor to define the width and height of a new contents frame. (See page 44 for further information on placing text files.)

4 If you used the default TOC paragraph styles you can edit them to format the table of contents as required.

You do not need to select the existing table of contents text frame before you regenerate the table of contents.

If there is overset text in your document when you generate a table of contents for the first time, or when you regenerate the table of contents, you get a warning prompt asking if you want to include any instances of paragraphs marked for inclusion that occur in the overmatter:

See pages 193–196 for further information on working with the Book palette.

5 A table of contents becomes out of date if you make changes in the document that affect content entries. To regenerate a table of contents, choose Layout>Table of Contents. This takes you back into the Table of Contents dialog box. In the Options area, select the Replace Existing Table of Contents checkbox; then click OK. A message box appears to indicate that the table of contents has been updated. Click OK. InDesign regenerates the table of contents and flows it back into the existing table of contents text frame.

6 To generate a table of contents for an entire book, make sure you have the Book palette visible, with the correct book tab selected. When you create a table of contents for a book, you may well locate the table of contents in its own InDesign document with other front matter such as disclaimers and copyright statements. Working in the document where you want to locate the table of contents, choose Layout>Table of Contents. Select the required table of contents style from the TOC Style pop-up; then check that all other settings are what you require. Make sure that the Include Book Document checkbox in the Options area is selected; then click OK to generate the table of contents text file.

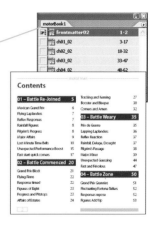

Creating an Index Entry

If you do not highlight text, or have the Text insertion point located in a text frame, the New Page Reference command in the Index palette is not available.

Use the Topic option when you want to create a topic or category in the index, for example, "Color". Typically, topics in an index do not have a page number reference associated with them. Depending on the complexity and extent of your publication, it can be a good idea to create a list of topics for the index before you begin to create individual index entries.

If you do not highlight words, but click to place the text insertion point in your text, when you choose the New Page Ref command, the level 1 index entry field is empty. You then have to create the text for the entry manually.

The Number Style Override allows you to control the exact appearance of the page numbers in your index. You need to set up Character Styles for the publication in order to use this feature. You can then choose a Character Style from the pop-up list.

To create an index, you first need to create the individual index entry references; then you can generate the index as a new text file, which you can format and edit to meet your requirements.

1 To create an index entry, choose Window>Type & Tables>Index (Shift+F8), to show the Index palette if it is not already showing.

Working with the Type tool, click to place the Text insertion point, or highlight the word or words you want to include in the index entry.

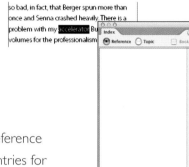

2 In the Index palette, click the Reference Mode button to create index entries for the index. (Click the Topic Mode button to create topics in the index.)

3 Choose New Page Ref from the Index palette menu (▶), or click the Create a New Index Entry button (▣) at the bottom of the Index palette.

4 The highlighted word appears in the Level 1 text field of the New Page Reference dialog box.

5 Choose a page numbering option for the index reference from the Type pop-up list. This option determines what page number or page number range appears with the index reference.

Index markers, visible when you choose Type>Show Hidden Characters, are inserted in the text when you create an index entry:

If you delete the index marker, the index reference is removed from the Index palette.

Hold down Ctrl/ Command and click the Expand/ Collapse triangle for an index section to show all subentries in that section.

To delete an index entry, click on the entry in the Index palette to select it; then click the Wastebasket icon at the bottom of the palette.

Only begin to structure and build your index when the text content is unlikely to change very much. If you start working on your index too early, changes, such as deleting chunks of text, may affect indexing you have already done.

6 Click OK to add the page reference to the Index palette.

7 Repeat the above process for every word you want to include in the index.

Viewing and Managing Index Entries

Use the Index palette to check, manage and edit the index as you continue to work on it.

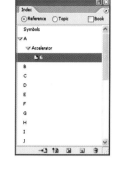

1 Click the expand/collapse triangle to show/hide the index entries in each alphabetic section. Alphabetic sections that do not contain index entries do not have an expand/collapse triangle.

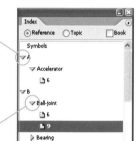

2 Click the expand/collapse button for an index entry to show/hide its page number reference.

3 Click a page number reference entry in the palette, and then click the Go to Selected Marker button (→🗐), at the bottom of the palette, to scroll the page and position the Text insertion point at the index entry marker in the text.

4 Choose Update Preview from the Index palette menu, or click the Update Preview button (↑🗐) to update information in the Index palette. You may need to do this, for example, if you have made edits to the text that result in index entry markers moving to different pages.

5 Working in Reference Mode, double-click either an index entry, or the index entry page reference, to edit settings in the Page Reference dialog box.

Generating an Index

At various stages as you build an index you will probably need to generate the index, in a text frame, to check and print it.

If you are generating an index for an entire book, in a separate index document, make sure that you include the index document in the book list.

1 To create an index, choose Generate Index from the Index palette menu, or click the Generate Index button (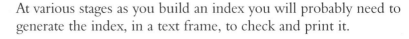) at the bottom of the palette.

2 In the Generate Index dialog box, change the title from Index if you want different wording for the title of your index. Use the Title Style pop-up list to choose a paragraph style to specify the appearance of the title.

See page 44 for further information on placing text.

3 Click OK. InDesign generates the index as a new text file and displays the Loaded text cursor. Use standard InDesign techniques to place the index text file. InDesign automatically generates paragraph styles (Index Level 1, Index Section Head, and Index Title), and uses these to format the index. If you have a multi-level index, InDesign generates Index Level 2 and 3 styles as well. You can edit these automatically generated styles, if necessary, to specify the exact appearance of the index.

To work with index entries for all documents included in a book, click the Book checkbox at the top of the Index palette.

To generate an index for an entire book, make sure you select the Include Book Documents checkbox in the Generate Index dialog box:

4 To regenerate an index after you make document changes that affect existing index entries, choose Generate Index from the palette menu. Make sure that the Replace Existing Index checkbox is selected, and then click OK.

Creating a Book

Use the Book palette to bring together a series of individual (but related) InDesign documents, such as the chapters of a book or technical manual, so that you can easily manage page numbering across the entire book, as well as create and maintain consistency of styles and color swatches. You can also create tables of contents and indexes for all documents included in a book list.

A book file has one style source document. The style source document is used to synchronize styles and colors to ensure consistency throughout the book.

1 To create a new book file, choose File>New>Book.

2 In the New Book dialog box, navigate to the folder where you want to save the book, using standard Windows/Mac techniques. Enter a name for the book. Notice that the extension for a book is ".indb". Click the Save button.

3 The Book palette appears on screen. The name of your book appears as a tab in the Book palette. You can have multiple book files open at the same time. You can now start adding individual InDesign documents to the book. InDesign documents you want to add do not need to be open to include them in the book list.

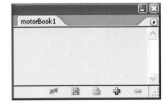

4 To add an InDesign document to the book list, either click the Add document button (⊕) at the bottom of the palette, or choose Add Document from the Book palette menu (▶).

5 Navigate to the file you want to add. Select it; then click Open. The file name appears in the book list. A page range for the document appears to the right of the entry in the book list. The first document you add becomes the style source. You can change the style source at any time (see page 196 for further information).

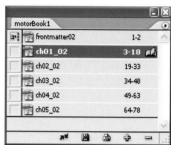

To print documents in a book, select the documents you want to print and then choose Print Selected Documents from the Book palette menu. To print the entire book, click in the blank area at the bottom of the palette so that no individual documents are selected, and then choose Print Book from the palette menu.

6 Continue to add documents to the book list until the book is complete. Provided that they are in the same folder, you can select more than one file at a time to add to the book list.

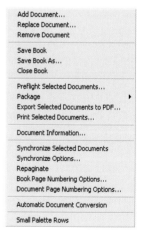

7 If you have more than one book open in the Book palette, choose Close Book from the palette menu to close the active book only. To close all books, click the Close button in the title bar of the Book palette.

The Save Book command saves changes to the book, not to the individual documents that make up the book.

8 You can save changes that you make to a book list (for example if you add or delete documents in the list, or change the order in which the documents occur) by choosing Save Book from the Book palette menu, or you can click the Save button (🖫) at the bottom of the palette.

Managing and Editing a Book

There is a variety of ways in which you can manage and edit a book list when preparing the publication.

1 To open a document included in the book list, double-click on the document name in the Book palette. An open document icon appears to the right of the file entry to indicate that the file is open.

2 To change the order of the documents in your book list, drag a document name up or down in the list. A thick black bar indicates the position to which the document will move when you release the mouse button. Page numbering updates automatically for all documents affected by the move.

3 To remove a document, click on the document name to select it; then click the Remove Document button (🔲) in the bottom of the palette, or choose Remove Document from the palette menu. Removing a file from the book list does not close the document if it is open.

4 In a book, automatic pagination is on by default. When you add, remove or reorder documents, pagination updates automatically so that pages remain numbered sequentially. This also happens if you add or remove pages within documents that are part of a book. To turn off automatic pagination, choose Book Page Numbering Options from the Palette menu; then deselect the Automatic Pagination checkbox.

Synchronizing a Book

The Style Source is the master file that is used to update other book files when you synchronize the book. The first document you add to the book palette automatically becomes the style source, indicated by the Style Source icon that appears in the left-hand column of the Book palette, next to the file name entry.

Use the Synchronize command to copy styles and color swatches from the style source document to the selected documents in the Book palette.

Styles or color swatches with identical names are updated in the selected documents to match the style source. You can use the Synchronize Options dialog box to control which sets of attributes are copied.

Styles and swatches in the style source that are not present in the selected documents are added to them.

Styles and swatches in the selected documents that are not in the style source are left unchanged.

1 To change the style source status to another document in the list, click the Style Source box in the column to the left of the document icon. The Style Source icon moves to the file. There can be only one style source file in a book.

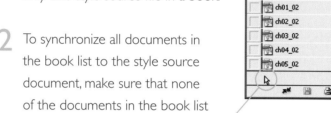

2 To synchronize all documents in the book list to the style source document, make sure that none of the documents in the book list is selected. To do this, either click in the blank area of the Book palette below the list of documents, or hold down Ctrl/Command and click any selected documents in the list. Choose Synchronize Book from the Book palette menu, or click the Synchronize button ( ) at the bottom of the palette.

3 To synchronize specific documents to the style source, select the documents; then choose Synchronize Selected Documents from the Book palette menu, or click the Synchronize button.

4 To control which settings you synchronize, select Synchronize Options from the palette menu. Click the checkboxes to deselect any settings you do not want to synchronize.

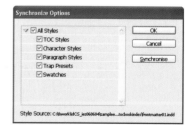

Printing and Exporting

As you build your documents in InDesign you will need to print copies for proofing purposes. This chapter shows you how to print proof copies to an inkjet or laser printer.

The chapter also shows you how to export documents as Adobe Acrobat PDF files, and covers the basics of tagging InDesign page items and exporting documents as XML.

Covers

Chapter Fourteen

Printing a Composite

InDesign supports printing to both PostScript® (Level 2 and 3) and non-PostScript printers (such as low-cost, color inkjet printers).

When you print a composite, all colors or shades in the document are printed on one sheet of paper. Printing from InDesign follows standard Windows and Mac principles.

1   To print a composite proof, choose File>Print. Select your printer from the Printer pop-up menu. Click printing categories in the categories list to create settings for each in turn. Enter the number of copies you want to print. In the Pages area, make sure

Print settings you create for a document are saved with the document.

the All Pages radio button is selected to print all pages in the document, or click the Range button to print specific pages. Enter the page numbers you want to print in the Range entry field. To specify a continuous range of pages, enter numbers separated by a hyphen, e.g. 10-15. To specify individual pages, enter numbers separated by a comma, e.g. 3, 6, 12. You can combine both techniques, e.g. 1-4, 8, 10, 12-15.

Adobe recommends using the PostScript 5 (system) driver for Windows 2000 (with Service Pack 2 installed) and Windows XP, and the built-in driver for Mac OS X. You can get further information on recommended and supported PostScript printer drivers on the Adobe Web site.

2   Select checkboxes in the Options area as required if you want to print page elements that do not normally print: non-printing objects, blank pages or non-printing guides.

3   Select the Setup category to set options for Paper Size, Orientation and Scale. As you make changes to these settings, the Preview area updates to give a visual preview of how the InDesign page will print on the selected paper size. Keeping an eye on the Preview can save you from printing with inappropriate settings.

...cont'd

Click the Save Preset button to save the current print settings as a preset, which you can then select from the Print Preset pop-up when you need to reuse the same settings.

Some print settings can be accessed through the printer's own dialog box as well as the InDesign Print dialog box. Where settings are duplicated, it is recommended that you use the InDesign settings, rather than the printer's settings.

If you are printing to a PostScript printing device, make sure you use the latest printer driver for your printer. Refer to the operating manual for complete information on setting up your printer correctly.

Controls for setting high-end print features such as color separations, Color Management and OPI settings are not available for non-PostScript language printers.

If the page size of your document is larger than the paper size you want to print on, you can use the Scale to Fit option. InDesign scales the page, and any printer's marks and bleed, to fit onto the selected paper size.

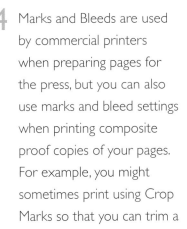

4 Marks and Bleeds are used by commercial printers when preparing pages for the press, but you can also use marks and bleed settings when printing composite proof copies of your pages. For example, you might sometimes print using Crop Marks so that you can trim a page to its final cut page size for proofing purposes. Bear in mind that if you select any of the Marks and Bleed options, these add to the overall size of the printed area and, as a result, not all page marks and bleed objects may fit on your chosen page size.

5 In the Output category, leave the Color pop-up set to Composite RGB to print a color composite proof. Select Composite Gray to print a grayscale version of the document. If you are printing to a PostScript output device, you can choose Separations from the

Print settings you create in the Print dialog box are saved with the document.

If you have introduced transparency effects into your document, by using drop shadows, feathering or the Transparency palette itself, you need to consider which Transparency Flattener setting to use. To print transparent effects, InDesign divides overlapping areas into discrete segments, which are output as either vector or rasterized areas. The transparency flattener setting controls the balance between vector and bitmap (rasterized) information used to output the transparent areas of the document.

Always advise your printer or service provider that you are using transparent effects in InDesign and ask for their recommendation as to which Flattener preset you should choose.

Print service providers can find further information on transparency output issues on the Print Service Provider Resource pages of the Adobe Solutions Network website.

Color pop-up. You can then control advanced output settings such as Trapping, halftone screen settings and which inks print.

6   In the Images area of the Graphics category, the Send Data pop-up menu allows you to choose quality settings for images in your document. Leave this on Optimized Subsampling for a basic composite proof. For a PostScript printer, you may need to download fonts to the printer if you have used fonts in the document that are not resident on the printer itself. Leave the download pop-up set to Complete.

7   In the Advanced category, choose a Transparency Flattener setting from the Preset pop-up if you have used effects such as Drop Shadow, Feathering or the Transparency palette.

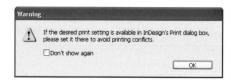

8   Click the Setup button to access the printer's own print settings dialog box. InDesign displays a warning box, which recommends that where possible you use settings from the InDesign Print dialog box, rather than from the printer's dialog box. Refer to your printer's instruction manual for information on the options available with your printer.

9   Click Print when you are satisfied with your settings.

Preflight

Preflight is an industry standard term for checking a document for problems before sending it to print.

It is good practice to preform a preflight check before sending a document to your printer, exporting to PDF, or using the Package command. The preflight check can alert you to possible problems, such as RGB images, missing fonts and the use of external or third-party plug-ins.

Use the Find Font dialog box with care and, if you replace fonts, check all pages carefully for changes in line endings that can occur when you substitute fonts.

1 To preflight a document, choose File>Preflight. An alert triangle (⚠) appears on the Summary screen if InDesign detects problems in any of the categories. For detailed information click the category label in the list on the left.

See pages 93–95 for further information on updating modified images and relinking to images.

2 If there are missing fonts, click the Find Font button to open the Find Font dialog box, which allows you to search for and replace missing fonts.

Preflight does not detect RGB images embedded in placed EPS, Adobe Illustrator or Macromedia FreeHand files.

3 Links and Images is a useful category that allows you to check for instances of RGB color mode images, and also whether image links are correct and up to date. You can relink to files from the Preflight dialog box if necessary.

For Fonts, select the Show Problems Only checkbox to list fonts used in the document that are not installed on your computer; fonts that have a screen font, but not the corresponding printer font; and fonts that cannot be embedded in PDF or EPS files due to licensing restrictions.

4 Colors and Inks allows you to check for duplicate color definitions for spot colors. Print Settings provides a summary of existing print settings for the document. External plug-ins provides a useful alert to potential issues that might arise if the document relies on external or third-party plug-ins to output correctly.

5 Click the Report button to generate a plain text file (.txt) of the preflight information, which you can open in any text editor.

Package

The Package command is useful when you are preparing to send a document to your printer or service bureau. Packaging facilitates the process of bringing together the InDesign document and all image files and fonts used in the document – copying them into a folder, which you can then send.

To create a package for a Book publication you must choose Package Book from the Book palette menu. If you have selected individual documents in the Book palette, you can choose Package Selected Documents.

1 Choose File>Package. As part of the packaging process, InDesign automatically runs the Preflight utility. You get a warning alert if

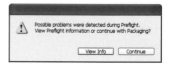

InDesign detects any potential problems. You can choose to view the Preflight dialog box, or continue with the packaging.

2 If you click Continue, the Printing Instructions box appears. Use this, if necessary, to supply contact details and any specific printing instructions to the printer. The Printing

Instructions are saved into the package folder as a plain text file that can be opened by any text editing application.

3 In the Package Publication dialog box, specify where you want to save the package folder, and specify the name for the package folder in the Folder Name entry box.

4 Select options to specify the set of items to be copied into the package folder.

Copy Fonts (Except CJK) – copies the fonts required to print the document, without copying a complete font family or typeface unless necessary.

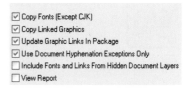

Copy Linked Graphics – is an important option, as the original image file holds the complete file information needed for high-resolution printing. If you do not copy linked graphics to the folder, the document will print using low-resolution screen versions of images – typically producing poor-quality results. InDesign automatically creates a sub-folder named "Links" within the package folder when you select this option.

Update Graphic Links in Package – allows InDesign to rewrite the paths of links to the images it copies to the Links folder.

Use Document Hyphenation Exceptions Only – prevents the document from composing with the external user dictionary on the computer which opens the file. It can be important to select this option when sending the document to a printer/service bureau.

It is only necessary to select the Include Fonts and Links from Hidden Document Layers option if there are additional layers in the document that contain these elements.

5 Click the Package button to start the process of copying files as necessary to the package folder. The Font Alert appears to remind you about copyright of fonts. Click OK if you are satisfied that you are not breaking any copyright agreements for the fonts in the document. InDesign gathers the files into the specified folder.

Exporting to PDF

You can export an InDesign document as PDF (Portable Document Format), either for high-resolution printing, or for viewing using Acrobat Reader or Web browsers. This section examines how you export documents for on-screen viewing.

To get the best results when you view a PDF file exported from InDesign, use Acrobat reader 5.0 or later.

One major advantage of using PDF format is that it preserves the layout and content of the original InDesign document without the viewer needing to have access to InDesign itself. The other advantage is the small file sizes that PDF offers.

1 To export a file in PDF format, finalize your layouts and save the file. Choose File>Export. Choose Adobe PDF from the Save as Type pop-up (Windows), or Format pop-up (Mac). Specify a location where you want to save the file, using standard Windows/Mac techniques. Enter a name for the file, and then click Save.

2 In the Export PDF dialog box, select an option from the Adobe PDF Preset pop-up menu. Each preset specifies a set of predefined settings, optimized for a particular PDF output requirement. For example, [Press Quality] is intended for PDF files that will be printed on imagesetters or platesetters as high-quality final output. [Press Quality] typically preserves the maximum amount of information contained in the original InDesign document. [Smallest File Size], on the other hand, creates PDF files that are suitable

To import a PDF Preset supplied to you by your printer or output bureau, choose File>PDF Export Presets>Define. In the PDF Export Presets dialog box, click the Load button, and then navigate to the Presets file. Click on the Presets file to select it, and then click Open:

...cont'd

If you are preparing PDFs for commercial printing, check with your printer or output bureau about which Compatibility and Standard settings to use.

for on-screen viewing, for example on the World Wide Web. [Smallest File Size] downsamples image quality and compresses file information to create a file that is as small as possible. When you choose one of the presets, settings in the PDF export categories change according to the preset you choose.

3 In the General category, specify whether you want to export all the pages in the document, or a specified range of pages. In the Options area, select the View PDF After Exporting checkbox, to launch the default PDF viewer, typically Acrobat Reader, so that you can check the result.

Select the Spreads checkbox if you want left- and right-hand pages to be downloaded as a single spread. Use this option so that the PDF viewer displays spreads as if you are reading a magazine or book. Do not select the Spreads option for print publishing, as this can prevent your commercial printer from imposing the pages.

4 Compression settings are controlled initially by the preset you choose. Again it is important if you are preparing a PDF for commercial printing that you consult with your printer or output bureau about which preset to choose, and only make changes to compression settings as directed.

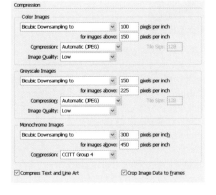

After you choose a preset, if you select a category from the list on the left, and then make changes to the predefined settings, "(modified)" is appended to the preset name. If you use a set of PDF options on a regular basis, you can save your own custom settings as a Preset. (For information on this see page 206.)

5 You typically do not need to create Marks and Bleeds settings for PDFs intended for on-screen viewing. For PDFs intended for print, ask your printer or output bureau about the options you should set to meet their printing specifications.

Your commercial printer or output bureau may well have a PDF Preset that they can supply, which defines PDF export specifications to meet their specific requirements.

6 In the Output category settings, if you are using the [Smallest File Size] preset, leave Color options set to the defaults.

7 In the Advanced category, for printed final output, the

Transparency Flattener setting can be important; it can affect the quality of printed output if you have used effects such as Drop Shadow, Feathering or the Transparency palette itself. Always inform your printer the first time you use a new transparency effect, and check with them as to which Flattener setting you should choose.

If required, choose Security from the categories list. Use the Security settings to control the degree of access that a viewer has for the PDF file. For example, you can set a Document Open Password so that only viewers who know the password are able to view the file. In the Permissions area, you can select the Use a password... checkbox to control editing and printing rights for the PDF.

8 Click Export when you are satisfied with the settings. If you chose the View PDF after Export option in the General category, Acrobat Reader launches and displays the exported PDF file.

Saving a Preset

If you use a custom set of PDF settings on a regular basis it is worth creating your own preset.

When you create PDF settings and then export the PDF file, the settings you created remain in force for other InDesign documents until you change them again.

1 To create a PDF preset, apply the settings you want in each of the PDF Export categories. Click the Save Preset button. Enter a name for the preset in the Save Preset dialog box, and click OK. The custom preset is now available in the Presets pop-up menu.

Creating XML Tags

Before you can export content from InDesign as an XML file, you must create or import the XML tags you want to use, and then apply the tags to blocks of content in your InDesign document.

Use the Tags palette to create or import tags. The Root element, which appears by default, is the topmost level of your XML structure. The Root element can be renamed, but not deleted or moved.

To show the Tags palette if it is not already showing, choose Window>Tags.

1   To create a new tag, choose New Tag from the Tags palette menu, or click once on the New Tag button (▣) located at the bottom of the palette.

2   Enter a name for the tag. An alert appears if you include a space or any other restricted character, such as a " / " (forward slash), in the tag name.

To edit an existing tag name or color, double-click the tag name in the Tags palette, or choose Tag Options from the Tags palette menu.

3   Choose a highlight color for the tag from the Color pop-up menu. The highlight color is used when you choose View>Structure>Show Tagged Frames or View>Structure>Show Tag Markers to visually identify your tagging in the InDesign environment. (See page 208 for further information). Click OK.

Importing XML tags

InDesign allows you to import XML tags from an XML file or from another InDesign file.

To import tags, choose Load Tags from the Tags palette menu. Navigate to the XML or InDesign file. Select the file; then click Open. The imported XML tags appear in the palette.

Applying Tags

In InDesign you can tag graphic frames, text frames, individual paragraphs within frames, and even inline frames.

When you tag a page item such as a text frame, an entry for the element appears in the Structure pane. (See page 210 for information on working with the Structure pane.)

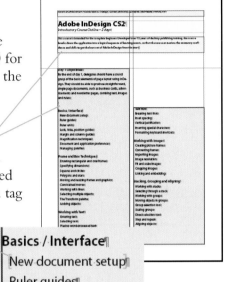

When you tag a page frame, a colored overlay is visible on the frame when View>Structure>Show Tagged Frames is selected. When you tag a range of selected text, colored text markers appear around the element when View>Structure>Show Tag Markers is selected.

1. To tag a text or graphic frame, select the Selection tool; then click on the frame to select it. Click on a tag in the Tags palette. To tag a frame that is part of a group, select it with the Direct Selection tool. Alternatively, you can drag a selected text or graphic frame into the Structure pane, release the mouse, and then select a tag name from the list that appears.

2. To tag selected text or a paragraph within a text frame, use the Type tool to highlight the range of text you want to tag; then click a tag in the Tags palette. You can only apply a tag to text within a text frame if the text frame itself is already tagged. A warning prompt appears if you attempt to tag text within a text frame that is not tagged; you can choose a tag for the frame from the warning prompt dialog box.

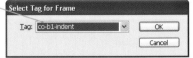

3 When you apply a tag to a range of text within a text frame, the new element becomes a child element of the parent text frame. This is indicated by the indent in the Structure pane.

4 To remove a tag from an item, select the tagged frame or text; then click the Untag button in the Tags palette.

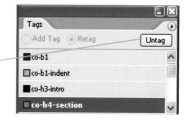

Retagging Page Items

1 To change the tag for a text or graphic frame, use the Selection tool, click on the frame to select it, and then click a different tag name in the palette.

2 To retag an individual paragraph, use the Type tool and click into the paragraph to place the Text insertion point. Make sure the Retag radio button in the top of the palette is selected, and then click on a different tag name.

XML Structure Pane

The Structure pane displays a hierarchical tree of the tagged page items or imported content. To show the Structure pane if it is not already showing, choose View>Structure>Show Structure (Ctrl/Command+Alt/option+1). Alternatively, click the Show/Hide Structure button (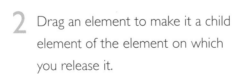) at the bottom of the InDesign window.

The entries that appear in the Structure pane are referred to as elements. If necessary, click the expand/collapse triangle to the left of Root to display any XML structure for the document. A blue diamond symbol on an element icon indicates that the element is associated with a page item.

You can reorder elements in the Structure pane to specify the sequence and hierarchy of page items in the XML file you export.

1 To reorder elements in the Structure pane, drag the element up or down. A thick black bar indicates the position to which the element will move when you release the mouse.

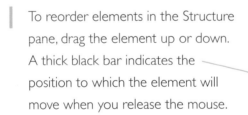

2 Drag an element to make it a child element of the element on which you release it.

3 When you select a tagged page item in the InDesign layout, the corresponding element in the Structure pane displays with an underline to indicate its selected status. If you select a child element, the parent element is also underlined.

Exporting XML

The purpose of XML is to separate content from formatting and layout positioning. After you have tagged page items you can then export the document to XML.

1 Choose File>Export. Use standard Windows/Mac techniques to specify the folder into which you want to export the XML file. Choose XML from the Save as Type pop-up (Windows), or Formats pop-up (Mac). Change the file name if required.

2 Click the Save button. In the General tab of the Export XML dialog box, you can select a DTD to associate with the XML file, if you imported one into the InDesign file; otherwise, the option is not available. Select the View XML Using checkbox; then select the browser or XML editor in which you want the XML file to appear after you export it. If you selected an element in the Structure pane before exporting, you can select the Export from Selected Element option to export the XML from that element.

3 If you include images in the XML structure, you can click the Images tab to specify the sub-folder into which the images are exported, and set options for optimizing images for the Web.

4 Click the Export button when you are satisfied with your settings. The XML appears in the application you selected in the General tab.

Snippets

A snippet is an XML file that represents content from an InDesign page. For example, you could save a series of headline, intro and body frames representing a magazine news story as a snippet.

You can easily re-use snippets in other pages or other documents.

Saving Snippets

You can also create an InDesign snippet by dragging selected frames onto the Windows or Mac desktop.

1. To create a snippet, use the selection tool to select a single frame or multiple frames.

2. Choose File>Export. Select InDesign Snippet from the Save as type pop-up (Windows), or Format pop-up (Mac).

3. Enter a name for the file; then click the Save button. Snippets save with an ".inds" file extension.

Adding Snippets to a Document

Snippets allow you to save and store content, formatting structure and tags quickly and conveniently as an XML file.

1. To add a snippet to a document, choose File>Place. Use standard Windows/Mac dialog box techniques to navigate to the snippet you want to place. Choose InDesign Snippet from the Files of type pop-up. Select the snippet name; then click the Open button, or double-click on the file name.

2. The snippet appears on the page with formatting, structure and content exactly as it was exported.

Transformations and Transparency

As well as the options available in the Control and Transform palettes, InDesign provides dedicated tools – the Rotate, Scale, Skew and Free Transform tools – for applying and controlling transformations to page objects. This chapter shows you how to use this set of tools. It also shows you how to change objects by adjusting transparency and by applying drop shadows and feathering.

Covers

Chapter Fifteen

The Rotate Tool

The Rotate tool, like the Scale and Skew tools, works around a point of origin – the point around which the transformation takes place. The point of origin marker appears when you have a selected object and you then click on the Rotate tool. You can reposition the point of origin marker if necessary.

When you are transforming objects or groups, the further away from the point of origin marker you position the transform cursor, the smoother the control you have over it.

1 To rotate an object, first select it with the Selection tool. Click on the Rotate tool. As soon as you select the Rotate tool, the point of origin marker (✛) appears on the object. The initial position of the marker is determined by the proxy reference point currently selected in the Control or Transform palette. Position the rotate cursor slightly away from the point of origin marker; then drag in a circular direction. Hold down Shift as you drag to constrain the rotation to increments of 45°.

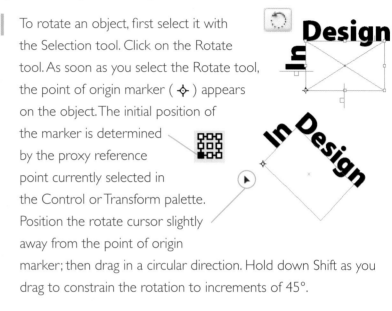

You can also reposition the point of origin marker by clicking on a proxy reference point in the Control or Transform palette:

2 To reposition the point of origin marker, with the Rotate tool selected, position your cursor on the marker; then drag it to another position. Alternatively, position your cursor at a different location, and then click. You can reposition the marker inside the selected object or anywhere on the page outside it.

Click the Preview button to see a preview of the transformation before you OK the dialog box.

3 To rotate using the Rotate dialog box, select an object using the Selection tool; then double-click the Rotate tool. Enter a rotation amount in the Angle entry field.

Enter a value from -360 to 360. Negative values rotate an object in a clockwise direction; positive values act counterclockwise. This rotates the object and its contents.

4 To rotate the object, but not its contents, deselect the Rotate Contents checkbox in the Rotate dialog box.

5 Click the Copy button instead of the OK button to create a rotated copy of the original object.

6 You can use the Rotate dialog box to create a circular rotation effect. To create this effect it is best to create a vertical and a horizontal ruler guide so that you can work easily around a center point. Start by creating the shape you want to rotate. Position it on the vertical guide above the center point. Make sure the shape remains selected. Select the Rotate tool. Position your cursor where the vertical and horizontal ruler guides meet. Hold down Alt/option, and click. This does two things: it sets the point of origin where you click, and it opens the Rotate dialog box. Enter a rotation angle, and then click the Copy button. Make sure the rotated object remains selected; then choose Object>Transform Again>Transform Again to repeat the transformation. Use the same command to continue repeating the transformation.

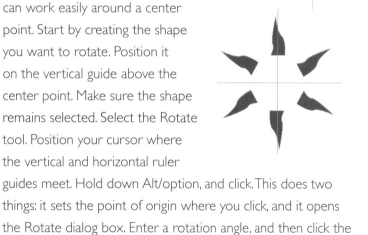

For this technique to work effectively, you need to enter a rotation angle that divides into 360°, for example 15, 30, 36 or 60:

You can use the keyboard shortcut Ctrl/ Command+Alt/ option+3 to repeat the Rotate or any other transformation.

The Scale Tool

You can scale objects manually using the Scale tool, or you can use the Scale dialog box. Like the Rotate and Skew tools, the Scale tool scales around a point of origin.

When you use any of the transformation tools, if you press and drag the mouse in one action, you see a blue bounding box that represents the result of the transformation. When you release the mouse button, the transformation is applied to the object. If you press the mouse button, but pause briefly before you begin to drag, you see a live preview of the transformation on the object.

1 To scale an object manually using the Scale tool, first select the object with the Selection tool. Then select the Scale tool. The point of origin marker appears on the object or group. The position of the marker is determined by the currently selected proxy reference point in the Control or Transform palette. (See page 214 for information on controlling the position of the point of origin marker.)

2 Position the Scale cursor slightly away from the point of origin marker; then start to drag. To scale the object in proportion, hold down Shift and start to drag at an angle of 45°. To scale the object horizontally only, hold down Shift and drag the cursor horizontally. To scale the object vertically only, hold down Shift and drag the cursor vertically.

3 To scale an object using the Scale dialog box, select the object using the Selection tool; then double-click the Scale tool. Either enter a Scale amount to scale the object in proportion, or select the Non-Uniform option and enter Horizontal and Vertical values to scale non-proportionally. Scale Content is selected by default. Deselect the option if you want to scale the object's frame but not its contents.

The Shear Tool

Use the Shear tool to slant or shear an object. The Shear tool obeys the same basic principles as the Rotate and Scale tools.

1 To Shear an object manually, first select the object with the Selection tool, and then select the Shear tool. The point of origin marker appears on the object or group. The position of the marker is determined by the currently selected proxy reference point in the Control or Transform palette. (See page 214 for information on controlling the position of the point of origin marker.)

2 Position the Shear cursor slightly away from the point of origin marker, and start to drag. Hold down the Shift key and drag at a 45° angle to constrain the shear. Hold down the Alt/option key as you shear to create a copy of the original object or group. You can use this technique to create shadow-like effects on objects.

3 To use the Shear dialog box, select an object or group with the Selection tool, and then double-click the Shear tool.

The Free Transform Tool

Unlike the Rotate, Scale and Skew tools, the Free Transform tool does not display a point of origin marker on the selected object when you select the tool. Using the Free Transform tool you can move, scale, rotate, reflect and shear objects. The tool's functionality is very similar to that of the equivalent tool in Photoshop and Illustrator.

For a text object, the corner handles become bold when you select it using the Free Transform tool:

TRANSFORM

1 To scale an object using the Free Transform tool, first select the object using the Selection tool; then select the Free Transform tool. Drag any selection handle to scale the object. Hold down Shift and drag a corner handle to scale the object in proportion. Hold down Alt/option and drag a handle to scale the object around its center point.

2 To rotate a selected object, select the Free Transform tool; then position your cursor slightly outside the object's bounding box. The cursor changes to the rotate cursor. Drag the cursor in a circular direction.

3 To reflect a selected object, select the Free Transform tool; then drag a handle through the opposite edge or handle.

4 To shear a selected object, select the Free Transform tool, start to drag any of the center side or center top handles, but not a corner handle, and then hold down Ctrl/Command as you continue to drag. Use the Shift key as you perform this procedure to constrain the effect. If you copy an object, reflect it and shear it, you can produce some interesting results.

Transparency Palette

Using transparency settings, you can allow underlying objects to show through other objects. You can apply transparency to selected objects, including graphic and text frames. You cannot apply transparency to individual text characters. Transparency affects the fill and stroke of an object equally.

An opacity setting of 100% means that the object is completely solid. An opacity setting of 0% makes an object completely transparent.

1   To set transparency for an object, select it using the Selection tool. Choose Window>Transparency (Shift+F10) to show the Transparency palette if it is not already showing.

2   Either drag the Opacity slider, or enter an Opacity amount. The lower the setting, the more transparent an object becomes.

3   To overlay text on a faded, or knocked-back, area of an image, place text in a separate text frame on top of a frame with reduced opacity, so that the opacity setting is not applied to the text.

Drop Shadows and Feathering

Using the Drop Shadow or Feathering option also adds transparency to a page. When you use transparency settings, the Transparency Flattener setting you choose when printing or exporting PDFs can affect the final output.

1   To apply a drop shadow to an object, select the object using the Selection tool. Choose Object>Drop Shadow. Select the Preview checkbox so that you can see the result of settings you create in the dialog box before you OK it.

2   Select the Drop Shadow checkbox to switch on the effect with default settings applied. Select a blend mode from the Mode pop-up menu. Use the Opacity setting to change the transparency of the shadow.

When you start using drop shadows, unless you have experience of using blend modes in an application such as Adobe Photoshop, leave the Mode pop-up set to Multiply.

3   Use the X/Y Offset values to move the shadow horizontally/vertically relative to the selected object. Increase the Blur setting to soften the shadow and produce a more subtle effect. Select a color from the existing swatches list to specify a color for the shadow. Add a small amount of Noise to make the effect more realistic.

To apply a drop shadow to text, make sure the text frame does not have a fill color; select the text frame with the Selection tool, and then choose Object>Drop Shadow.

4   Feathering softens the edge of an object, fading it to transparent over a specified distance. To feather a selected object, choose Object>Feather. Select the Feather checkbox to switch on the effect. Enter a Feather Width amount to control the amount of fade. Choose an option from the Corners pop-up to change the nature of the effect.

Paths and the Pen and Pencil Tools

Use the Pen tool to create open and closed paths consisting of any combination of curves and straight line segments. Use tools in the Pen tool group to add and delete points, and to convert points from smooth to corner and vice versa. Use the Pencil group of tools to create freeform open and closed paths and to manipulate paths.

Covers

Chapter Sixteen

Points and Paths

Use the Direct Selection tool to select and edit points to define the exact shape of a path:

In InDesign, the shape of all basic objects, including frames and shapes drawn with the Pen and Pencil tools, is defined by a path. You can manipulate paths and points in a variety of ways to achieve precisely the shape you need.

Paths and Points

A path consists of two or more anchor points joined together by curve or straight line segments. The Pen tool allows you to position anchor points precisely where you want them as you create the path. You can also control which type of point you create – smooth or corner. The Pencil tool creates freeform paths, which are formed as you drag the cursor.

You create a closed path with the Pen tool when you click back at the start point.

Open and Closed Paths

Using the Pen and Pencil tools you can create open and closed paths. Objects such as rectangles and ovals, as well as text and graphic frames, are closed paths.

The word "point" is often used to mean anchor point. Direction points are always referred to in full.

Smooth and Corner Points

There are two kinds of points that you need to understand in order to work creatively and precisely with paths: Smooth points connect two curve segments in a smooth, continuous curve; Corner points allow an abrupt, sharp change in direction at the point. You can create paths consisting of both kinds of points as you draw them, and you can convert points from one type to the other using the Convert Direction Point tool.

The center point that appears when you select a path with the Selection tool is not an editable point. It simply indicates the center of the bounding box that represents the outer boundary of the path.

Direction Points

When you click on an anchor point connecting curve segments, using the Direct Selection tool, one or two direction points (depending on the type of point) appear, attached to their associated anchor point by direction lines. Direction points control the length of a curve segment and the direction of the curve segment as it leaves the point.

The Pen Tool

The Pen tool is the most versatile and precise tool you can use for defining shapes accurately. You can use the Pen tool to create straight line segments, curve segments, or a mixture of both, with precise control over the positioning and type of anchor points. The Pen tool can create open or closed paths.

Straight Line Segments

1 To create a straight line segment, select the Pen tool, position your cursor where you want the line to start, and then click. This sets the first anchor point, and defines the start point of the path.

Hold down Shift, and click with the Pen tool to constrain straight line segments to horizontal, vertical or increments of 45 degrees.

2 Move the cursor to a new position. (Do not press and drag; simply reposition the cursor.) Click. This sets the second anchor point. A straight line segment is created between the two points. Repeat the procedure to create the number of straight line segments you need.

The screen shots used to illustrate points about the Pen tool show the path only – no strokes are applied.

3 To finish drawing the path, position your cursor back at the start point (a small circle appears with the Pen tool cursor), and then click to create a closed path.

4 Alternatively, click the Pen tool again (or any other tool in the Toolbox) to create an open path. Clicking another tool indicates that the path is complete and that you have finished adding segments. You can also choose Edit>Deselect All (Ctrl/Command+Shift+A) to complete the path.

Curve Segments

1. To create curve segments, with the Pen tool selected, position your cursor where you want the path to start. Press and drag. This action sets the first anchor point and defines its associated direction points. (See pages 226–230 for further information on how direction points control the shape of curves.)

2. Release the mouse button. An anchor point and two direction points are visible.

3. Move the Pen tool cursor to a new position. Press and drag to set another anchor point and to define its associated direction points. Setting the second anchor point also defines the curve segment between the first and second anchor points.

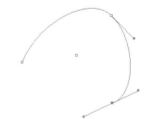

4. Repeat the procedure to create as many curve segments as you require.

5. To finish drawing the path, position your cursor back at the start point (a small loop appears with the Pen tool cursor); then click to create a closed path.

6. Alternatively, click the Pen tool again (or any other tool) to create an open path. You can also choose Edit>Deselect All (Ctrl/Command+Shift+A), to complete the open path.

To make adjustments to a path while you are drawing it, hold down Ctrl/Command to temporarily access the Direct Selection tool. Make changes as necessary; then release the Ctrl/Command key to resume drawing the path.

To add more segments to an existing path, select an end point using the Direct Selection tool. Select the Pen tool; then either click on the selected end point, or press and drag on the end point. Move the cursor to a new position and continue to click, or press and drag, to add segments to the path.

Adding and Deleting Points

You can add points to an existing path to achieve the exact shape you require, and you can delete points from a path to simplify it, if necessary. You can add and delete anchor points using the Add or Delete Anchor Point tool, or using the Pen tool.

As a general rule of thumb, the fewer points there are in a path the less complex it is and the quicker it processes at output. Very complex paths can sometimes cause printing problems.

1 To add an anchor point to an existing path or frame, select the Add Anchor Point tool. Position your cursor on the path (it doesn't matter whether the path is selected or not); then click to add a point. Points added to curve segments automatically appear with direction points. Points added to straight line segments do not have direction points.

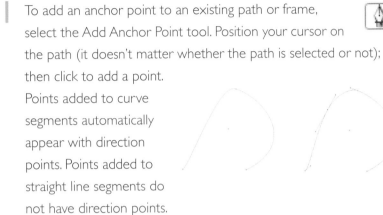

You can also add and delete points on basic shapes such as rectangles, ovals and frames.

2 To delete an existing anchor point, select the path with either the Selection tool or the Direct Selection tool. Select the Delete Anchor Point tool. Position your cursor on a point; then click to delete the point. The path redraws without the point.

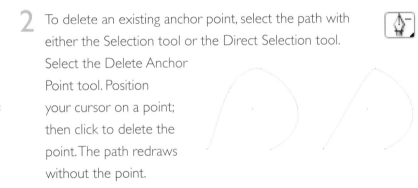

3 To add an anchor point with the Pen tool, first select a path with one of the selection tools. Select the Pen tool. Position your cursor on the path. A plus appears with the Pen tool cursor ( ). Click to add an anchor point.

4 To delete an anchor point with the Pen tool, first select a path. Position the Pen cursor on an existing anchor point. A minus symbol appears with the cursor ( ). Click to delete the point.

Selecting and Manipulating Points

You will usually need to select and manipulate anchor points and direction points to fine-tune the path you are working with. Use the Direct Selection tool to work on paths in this way.

Editing Anchor Points

To select an anchor point, select the Direct Selection tool. Click on a path to select it. The path becomes highlighted and the anchor points that form the shape appear as hollow squares. Click on an anchor point to select it. The point becomes solid. If the anchor point connects curve segments, direction points will also appear, connected to the anchor point by direction lines.

When you have selected an anchor point using the Direct Selection tool, you can press the Up/Down/Left/Right arrow keys on the keyboard to nudge the points in small steps. Choose Edit>Preferences>Units & Increments (Windows), or InDesign>Preferences>Units & Increments (Mac), if you want to change the Cursor Key increment from the default setting.

2 To change the shape of the path, drag the point to a new location. Hold down Shift and drag the point, if you want to constrain its movement to vertical, horizontal or multiples of 45 degrees.

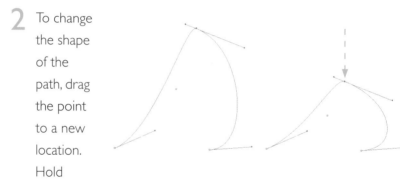

Editing Direction Points

Anchor points that have curve segments entering or leaving the point have associated direction points. Direction points control the length and shape of the curve segments. Continue working with the Direct Selection tool to edit direction points.

To edit the direction points associated with a point, first select a point that has curve segments entering or leaving it. The anchor point becomes

solid and the associated direction points appear, connected to the anchor point by direction lines.

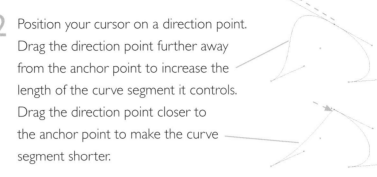

2 Position your cursor on a direction point. Drag the direction point further away from the anchor point to increase the length of the curve segment it controls. Drag the direction point closer to the anchor point to make the curve segment shorter.

Hold down Shift as you drag a direction point to constrain it to multiples of 45 degrees.

3 Drag a direction point in a circular direction around the anchor point to change the angle at which the curve segment enters or leaves the anchor point. The result is to change the shape of the curve segment. A preview of the change appears as a blue line as you drag the direction point.

Smooth and Corner Points

Understanding the difference between smooth and corner anchor points will give you complete control over the shape of paths.

Smooth Points

A smooth point maintains a smooth, continuous transition or curve from the incoming to the outgoing curve segments, through the anchor point.

Select the Direct Selection tool, then click on a smooth anchor point. Two direction points appear, connected to the anchor point by direction lines. Position your cursor on a direction point; then press and drag in a circular direction around the point. As you move the direction point, the opposite direction point moves like a balance, keeping both direction points perfectly aligned. If you move the direction point further away from or closer to the anchor point, the distance of the opposing direction point does not change.

Corner Points

Use corner points to create a sharp change in direction at the anchor point.

Click on a corner point to select it. Two direction points appear, connected to the anchor point by direction lines. Drag a direction point in a circular direction around the anchor point and/or move the direction point closer to or further away from the anchor point. The opposite direction point does not move: for corner points, each direction point works completely independently of the other.

Converting Points and Cutting Paths

The Convert Direction Point tool can convert a smooth point to a corner point and vice versa, and it can also be used to retract direction points or create smooth points.

Converting Smooth to Corner

1 To convert a smooth point to a corner point, select the point using the Direct Selection tool. Select the Convert Direction Point tool. Position your cursor on one of the direction points; then press and drag. The point becomes a corner point – each direction point moves independently of the other.

2 If you are going to make further changes to the direction points to fine-tune the curves, it is good practice (although not essential) to reselect the Direct Selection tool, rather than continuing to work with the Convert tool.

Converting Corner to Smooth

1 To convert a corner point to a smooth point, select a corner point using the Direct Selection tool. Select the Convert Direction Point tool. Position the cursor on the anchor point (not a direction point); then drag off the point to convert the point to a smooth point and to define the shape of the smooth curve.

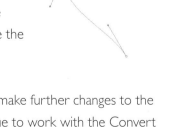

2 Reselect the Direct Selection tool to make further changes to the point or direction point. If you continue to work with the Convert tool on the same point, or its direction points, you will undo the results of Step 1.

Retracting Direction Points

To retract both direction points for either a smooth or a corner point, first select the point with the Direct Selection tool. Select the Convert Direction Point tool. Position your cursor on the anchor point; then click to retract the direction points. The incoming and outgoing curve segments are redrawn accordingly.

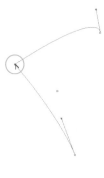

Converting a Retracted Point to a Smooth Point

To convert a retracted point to a smooth point, select a path with the Direct Selection tool. A retracted point is one that has no direction points associated with it when you click on it with the Direct Selection tool. Select the Convert Direction Point tool. Position your cursor on the retracted point; then drag off the point to create a smooth point and define the shape of the incoming and outgoing curve segments.

The Scissors Tool

Use the Scissors tool to split or cut a path anywhere along a curve or straight line segment, or at an anchor point.

To split an open or closed path, select the Scissors tool. Position your cursor at the point on the path where you want to cut it. (The path does not have to be selected, and you do not have to click on an existing anchor point.) Click. Two anchor points are created at the point at which you click.

Creating Text Outlines

Use the Create Outlines command to convert text into a series of compound paths. Treat the resultant paths as graphic objects. The Create Outlines command is useful for creating graphic effects with type, and is not normally used on smaller text sizes, such as body text.

1 To convert type to outlines, select the text frame with the Selection tool.

2 Choose Type> Create Outlines. Notice that the converted text still appears exactly the same as the

original text, but it now selects as an object – there are no In/Out ports on the bounding box.

3 Use the Direct Selection tool to edit the resultant paths.

4 To import an image into converted text, select the converted text object using the Selection tool. Choose File>Place. Use standard Windows/Mac techniques to navigate to the image file you want to place. Select the file name and then click Open. (See Chapter 6 for further information on working with images.)

The Pencil Tools

There are three tools in the Pencil tool group. The Pencil tool creates freeform open or closed paths, the Smooth tool creates smoother versions of paths, and the Erase tool erases portions of paths.

To add to an existing path using the Pencil tool, make sure the path is selected. Select the Pencil tool, position your cursor on either of the end points, and then drag.

1 To draw an open path with the Pencil tool, select the tool; then position your cursor on the page. The cursor changes to the Pencil tool cursor. Press and drag to create the path. A faint, dotted line indicates the shape of the path as you define it. When you release the mouse button, the path and the anchor points used to define its shape appear. The path takes on any fill and stroke attributes currently set.

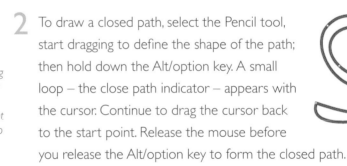

Double-click the Pencil tool and Smooth tool to access the Preferences dialog box for each tool. Fidelity settings control how closely the path conforms to the actual movement of the mouse: low settings tend to produce more detailed, angular paths; higher settings produce smoother curves. Smoothness settings control the amount of smoothing applied as you drag the cursor: low values produce less smooth, more angular results; higher values result in fewer anchor points and a smoother path.

2 To draw a closed path, select the Pencil tool, start dragging to define the shape of the path; then hold down the Alt/option key. A small loop – the close path indicator – appears with the cursor. Continue to drag the cursor back to the start point. Release the mouse before you release the Alt/option key to form the closed path.

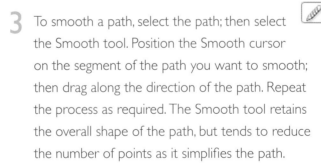

3 To smooth a path, select the path; then select the Smooth tool. Position the Smooth cursor on the segment of the path you want to smooth; then drag along the direction of the path. Repeat the process as required. The Smooth tool retains the overall shape of the path, but tends to reduce the number of points as it simplifies the path.

4 To erase portions of a path, select the path, and then select the Erase tool. Drag along the part of the path you want to erase.

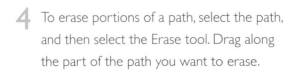

The Pathfinder Palette

Use the pathfinder commands to create new shapes from overlapping frames or shapes. The resultant paths can be interesting, complex shapes that it would be difficult to create any other way.

Choose Window>Object & Layout> Pathfinder to show the Pathfinder palette if it is not already showing.

Add

The Add pathfinder command creates a more complex shape from overlapping shapes. Add is useful when you want to create a complex shape with a unified outline or stroke from two or more basic shapes.

Typically, the pathfinder commands work by creating new shapes where existing paths overlap.

To add shapes, make sure you select at least two frames or basic shapes. Click the Add button on the Pathfinder palette, or choose Object>Pathfinder>Add. When frames or shapes have different fill and stroke attributes, the Add command applies the fill and stroke attributes of the frontmost object to the resultant shape.

Subtract

The Subtract command acts like a punch – shapes in front of the backmost object punch through and cut away areas of the backmost object where they overlap. The frontmost objects are deleted when you use the command. This is a useful technique for creating completely transparent areas in a shape.

You must have two overlapping shapes or frames selected to use commands in the Pathfinder palette.

To subtract shapes, make sure you select at least two frames or basic shapes. Click the Subtract button on the Pathfinder palette, or choose Object>Pathfinder>Subtract. When frames or shapes have different fill and stroke attributes, the backmost shape retains its fill and stroke attributes when you use the Subtract command.

You can create interesting effects using the Intersect command by applying it to a copy of the original shapes. Use the Paste in Place command to place the copied shapes directly on top of the original shapes. After you use the Intersect command on the copies, you can then recolor the resultant shape, which sits on top of the original shapes:

Intersect

The Intersect command creates a new shape where two shapes or frames overlap. Areas that do not overlap are removed. You can use the command for only two objects at a time. If you attempt to apply the command with more than two objects selected, a warning prompt indicates that you cannot proceed.

To intersect shapes, select two frames or basic shapes, click the Intersect button in the Pathfinder palette, or choose Object> Pathfinder>Intersect. The resultant shape retains the fill and stroke attributes of the frontmost object.

Exclude Overlap

The Exclude Overlap command makes the area where two or more frames or shapes overlap completely transparent.

To use Exclude Overlap, select two or more frames or basic shapes; then click the Exclude Overlap button in the Pathfinder palette, or choose Object>Pathfinder>Exclude Overlap. The resultant shape retains the fill and stroke attributes of the frontmost object.

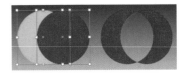

To use the Pathfinder commands on text, you must first convert it to outlines:

See page 231 for further information on converting text to outlines.

Minus Back

Minus Back is the opposite of the Subtract command. Objects behind cut away the frontmost object where they overlap.

To use Minus Back, select two or more frames or basic shapes; then click the Minus Back button in the Pathfinder palette, or choose Object>Pathfinder>Minus Back. The resultant shape retains the fill and stroke attributes of the frontmost object.

Index

A

Above Line Anchored Objects 118
Adding pages 142
Add Anchor Point tool 14, 225
Add pathfinder command 233
Adobe Bridge 16–18
Adobe Illustrator 7, 10, 87
Adobe Photoshop 7, 10, 87, 96
Align palette 21, 115
Align Stroke buttons 92
Align to Grid button 77
Alt key 10
Anchored Objects 117–118
Apple key 10
Apply Color button 14
Apply Gradient button 128
Apply None button 14
Auto-leading 65
Automatic Page Numbering 149

B

Baseline Grid 76
Baseline Shift 70
Bleed amount 33
Bleed and Slug 8
Books
  Add Document command 193
  Automatic pagination 195
  Document order 195
  Remove Document command 195
  Save Book command 194
  Style source document 193–194, 196
  Synchronizing 196
Book palette 185, 193
Bring to Front/Bring Forward 102
Button tool 14

C

Character palette 20, 65–70
Character styles 156
Check Spelling dialog box 130
Clipboard 42, 50
Clipping Paths 96–98
Color
  Applying Gradients 128
  Applying to Type 120
  Apply Color button 14
  CMYK mode 122
  Color Matching Systems 126
  Creating Tints 124
  Default Fill and Stroke button 14
  Deleting Swatches 123
  Editing 124
  Fill box 14, 120
  None 121
  Pantone 126
  Process 122–123
  RGB mode 122
  Spot 122–123
  Stroke box 14, 92, 120
Color Palette 125
Column guides 9
Command key 10
Context sensitive menus 10
Control palette 36–38
  Character Formatting Controls button 19
  Docking and Gripper Bar 19
  Paragraph Formatting Controls button 19
Convert Direction Point tool 14, 229
Copy command 42
Corner Effects 30
Create Outlines command 231
Cropping images 90
Cut and Clear commands 42

D

Delete Anchor Point tool 14, 225
Deleting pages 142
Dictionary dialog box 131
Direct Selection tool 35, 91, 96, 222–227
Discretionary Hyphens 79
Distributing Objects 116
Drag copy 33

T